Lessons Learned
Looking Back

Blessings!

Laura Z Sowers

Lessons Learned Looking Back

Strategies for Successful Living

TODD E. LINAMAN
& LAURA Z. SOWERS

BROADMAN
&HOLMAN
PUBLISHERS

Nashville, Tennessee

© 2001 by Todd E. Linaman and Laura Z. Sowers
All rights reserved
Printed in the United States of America

0-8054-2057-6

Published by Broadman & Holman Publishers, Nashville, Tennessee

Dewey Decimal Classification: 248
Subject Heading: CHRISTIAN LIVING

Unless otherwise noted, Scripture quotations are from The Holy
Bible, New International Version, © 1973, 1978, 1984. References
marked NASB are from the New American Standard Bible, © the
Lockman Foundation, 1960, 1962, 1963, 1968, 1971, 1972, 1973,
1975, 1977; used by permission. References marked NKJV are from
the New King James Version, © 1979, 1980, 1982, Thomas Nelson,
Inc., Publishers.

Library of Congress Cataloging-in-Publication Data
Linaman, Todd E., 1958–
        Lessons learned looking back : strategies for
    successful living / Todd E. Linaman and Laura Z. Sowers.
            p. cm.
    ISBN 0-8054-2057-6 (pbk.)
    1. Success—Religious aspects—Christianity. 2. Christian life.
    3. Spiritual life—Christianity. I. Sowers, Laura Z., 1950–
    II. Title.

    BV4598.3 .L56   2001
    248.4—dc21
                                                    00–063100
1 2 3 4 5 6 7 8 9 10 05 04 03 02 01

Contents

Foreword

BY DR. GARY D. CHAPMAN

"Experience is the best teacher." That's what my father told me. Far be it from me to question the wisdom of my father. However, I do see two problems with his sage advice. First, life is not long enough to experience everything. Dad lived eighty-six years. He grew up on the farm, did his time in the Navy, worked over thirty years for the same company, tried starting his own business twice, drove Fords, Chevrolets, and Buicks, and was a devout follower of Jesus. But even Dad did not have time to experience everything.

Second, there are some experiences I'd rather not have. When I was in college, I always hoped that I would not flunk out. When I learned to drive, I never wanted to experience an accident. I've never desired to experience cancer or Alzheimer's. Every time I fly, I have a sincere desire to land safely and not experience an airplane crash. So far, except for a minor auto accident, I've never had any of these experiences, and I am grateful. I know there are lessons to be learned by these experiences, but I'd prefer to learn them another way.

My grandfather was an alcoholic. He managed to work Monday through Friday, but it was a given that on Friday and Saturday nights, he would get drunk. On occasion, someone would knock at our door and inform my father that his father had fallen in a ditch on his way home from his "watering hole." At the age of ten I accompanied my father on his trip to retrieve my grandfather from the ditch and get him to his bed. That's the night I decided not to drink. I learned a valuable lesson from my grandfather's experience. Personally, I'm glad I didn't have to experience alcoholism to learn that lesson.

Since I won't live long enough to learn everything by personal experience and since I'd prefer not to have certain experiences, I'm left to learn some things from the experiences of others. Todd Linaman and Laura Sowers have enhanced that possibility with *Lessons Learned Looking Back: Strategies for Successful Living.* In this volume you will meet real people who have had struggles with real-life issues. Some made wise choices and some were not so wise, but we can learn from all. Entering into the lives of others, identifying with their emotions, observing thoughts, and evaluating their decisions is a fascinating way to learn.

This method of learning finds its precedent in biblical revelation. Paul said, "For everything that was written in the past was written to teach us, so that through endurance and the encouragement of the Scriptures we might have hope" (Rom. 15:4). Who has not learned by spending an hour with Moses, David, or Daniel? Contemporary followers of Christ also have lessons to teach, and the most powerful of those lessons are the lives they live. In the following pages, you will meet some of them, and I hope you will learn.

I guess my Dad was right. "Experience is the best teacher," and when I learn from the experience of others, it then becomes my experience.

Acknowledgments

Our sincere thanks to the many people who took the time to respond to our questionnaire and then to be further interviewed for this book. Your lessons learned looking back are the parables of our day. As the Lord has touched and taught you, we pray that your stories will do the same to those who read them. We weren't able to include all the many worthy stories, but we were blessed by them and by your willingness to share them. It should be noted that while all the incidents are true, many of the names and details have been changed to protect individual privacy.

We also want to thank Broadman & Holman Publishers for trusting us with the message of this book and for their fine work of editing, designing, and marketing.

FROM TODD LINAMAN:

I want to extend a very special thank you to my mother, Joyce Linaman, for faithfully sharing wisdom and insights from her own lessons learned. To Liz Bailey, my coworker and friend, thank you for your dedicated assistance and guidance. I also want to thank each member of my community group for their encouragement and unwavering prayer support.

Most importantly, I want to thank my wife Kendra and my children, Scott, Kristen, and Kathryn for all their love, patience, understanding, and prayers. You have all graciously sacrificed many hours together as a family to allow me to complete this work. I thank God daily for having blessed my life so richly with each of you. I love you.

FROM LAURA SOWERS:

A special thanks to my daughter, Cara Anne Ray, whose wise and prayerful suggestions on this book reflect an awesome woman after

God's own heart. Thanks also to my son-in-law Tim Ray, my precious son Marc, his wife, Cara Margaret, and their son Luke—your interest and prayers were a sustaining comfort. To my husband Craig, thank you for being my editor, critic, and greatest supporter—you encouraged and endured. Finally, I'd like to thank Jesus, the Anchor of my life and my soul.

Introduction

There is a saying which claims that "life is what happens while you're making other plans." Unfortunately, this is often true. The distractions of daily living can so thoroughly monopolize our attention that we neglect the important issues that determine the course of our lives. For instance, there are probably many areas in our lives that we have submitted to the Lord, while we may have unconsciously withheld others out of pride, shame, or thoughtless neglect.

God wants to be involved in every facet of our existence. To graphically illustrate this fact, we have covered a wide range of subjects in this book. We will see that when the Lord is allowed into every part of our lives, we are more likely to act with integrity and stability. Could you imagine purchasing a house and consenting to live in only a few rooms while others remained locked and off-limits? God longs for us to come to a point of loyalty and commitment where we surrender the keys to the secret chambers of our hearts, throw open the doors, and unreservedly invite him in. In so doing, we not only enter a profoundly rewarding relationship with the Lord; we greatly increase the likelihood of leading a fulfilled and purposeful life.

In our culture there is plenty of competition for our attention and loyalty. Clearly, it's difficult to be a twenty-first-century believer, but then the choice to follow God has never been an easy one. Jesus, in fact, assured us that we would be at odds with the world just as he was during his lifetime on earth. With our true citizenship established in heaven, we must keep in mind that we are tourists here, traveling on a limited passport until our hearts find their home with the Lord in heaven.

This situation is bound to create tension. The paradox of being in the world but not of the world guarantees we will experience conflict and hostility (see John 17:14). As children of God, our eternal security is fixed the instant we place our faith in Jesus, but translating our spiritual position and beliefs into the day-to-day actions of life is a long-term learning and growing process.

Many parents know the sorrow of watching a willful child stride headlong into bumps and bruises—we call it learning lessons in the school of hard knocks. Therefore, it's not difficult to imagine God's strong desire for our lessons to come as gently as possible rather than through painful and costly mistakes. The Bible and the leading of the Holy Spirit are our ultimate guides, but God has also given us the opportunity to learn from each other and make use of that wise counsel.

As God's kids, we become members of a vastly extended family that enables us to look outside our familiar environment and learn from our brothers and sisters in Christ. Just as in our immediate family, we watch those we love and admire and emulate their behaviors, learn from their mistakes, and pattern our goals based on observations of their lives.

Through the stories in this book, we can peek into believers' lives and see that God deals with us individually and teaches us creatively. Although he is faithful to meet us where we are when we earnestly seek him, our learning ultimately depends on our willingness to become pliable and teachable in his hands.

In this book, it is our goal to open the door to gentle learning. Among the many and varied lessons, we will see how individuals have:

- Resisted the pressures of the world to follow God's way,
- Looked for and discovered their unique God-directed goals,
- Trusted God in the face of overwhelming and frightening circumstances,
- Redefined their views of personal integrity and success,
- Experienced the joy of renewal in the wake of failure and regret, and
- Searched for and found the true meaning of life.

By way of these shared incidents we will see God's words translated into the walking, breathing life-experiences of others. It's comforting to be reminded that no one is perfect—we are all works in progress. The apostle Paul assured us that "he who began a good work in you will carry it on to completion until the day of Christ Jesus" (Phil. 1:6). Until that day, let us keep focused on our Lord, his ways, and our heavenly destination.

Our prayer for you is that these lessons learned looking back will enable you to face your future with courage and faith. We hope you will open your heart to a deeper awareness of God's all-encompassing love and will be encouraged by the experiences of imperfect people under the influence of a patient and perfect God.

1

Life Is an Open-Book Test

"For I know the plans I have for you," declares the LORD,
"plans to prosper you and not to harm you, plans to give
you hope and a future. Then you will call upon me
and come and pray to me, and I will listen to you."
JEREMIAH 29:11–12

"Take out a sheet of paper and a pencil for a pop quiz."
Do these words still send a shiver of dread and fear down your
spine?

Remember the students' typical response? "Not fair!" they
moaned. "If only we'd known we were going to be tested—we would
have studied—we would have been prepared. At least make it an
open-book test!"

As adults, we can look back on this scenario and immediately see
the immaturity of being taken off guard. After all, school and tests go
hand in hand! Failing to plan for such a situation was, indeed, planning to fail.

Yet we are still surprised and underprepared when normal life is
interrupted by the need to make a significant decision. Is it possible
that we haven't completely outgrown our naïveté? If we are yet making excuses and blowing our "pop quizzes," maybe it hasn't fully
occurred to us that we still need to be ready and equipped—the
school classroom has simply changed to the classroom of life.

If big (or small) decisions are sending us into a tailspin of random
choices or eleventh-hour searches for the elusive will and guidance of
God, we need to realign ourselves in a closer daily walk and communion with the Lord.

Wisdom and decision making are not reserved solely for those with a great deal of life experience. Although we certainly learn lessons through the events of our lives, sometimes those experiences carry a high price and leave us with deep regret. Our loving Father has made provisions to give wisdom to those who seek it and to teach it gently and generously.

> *If any of you lacks wisdom, he should ask God,*
> *who gives generously to all without finding fault,*
> *and it will be given to him. (James 1:5)*

We all long to make good decisions, but too often we fall short of the challenge. What does wisdom look like? How does God enable his people to make good decisions, avoid disasters, find peace in hard circumstances, change their faulty thinking, and reap blessings from hardships?

Sometimes we see the answers demonstrated in others' lives. Have you known people who seemed to consistently make wise and lasting choices in the defining decisions of life? Do these folks have unusual skills or a special inside track when it comes to choosing a mate, starting a business, and raising bright and respectful kids?

The man who walks with God always gets to his destination.
—UNKNOWN

In fact, there are several qualities and approaches that, when combined, greatly enhance our ability to make good decisions. Wisdom and good judgment are not singular qualities; they encompass obtaining and analyzing facts and the willingness to delay personal gratification by exercising self-discipline. Another important component is the ability to look squarely at our failures and learn from them. This, with God's help, prevents us from repeating past mistakes.

For many individuals, however, it isn't until they are caught in a maddening spiral of repeating situations and problems that it dawns on them that their old ways of doing things are not working. Finally, the utter frustration of exhausting their own efforts may bring them to a place where they're willing to listen, learn, and try something new.

A last resort? Perhaps. But sometimes it's the last key in the bunch that unlocks the door.

LITTLE CHOICES, BIG REWARDS

You may be wondering if it's possible or realistic to prepare in advance for good decision making. After all, how can you prepare when there are no options before you?

In reality, we overlook many pop-quiz decisions we make every day. Some are of minor consequence. It rarely matters whether we wear the red shirt or the plaid shirt. However, the quality and character of some daily decisions carry the seeds of major choices in the future.

For example, the daily choice to be an honest and diligent employee spares us the final-exam decision that would follow being fired for stealing or for performing poorly in our job. Likewise, as the following story shows, the choice to resist the enticements of a casual flirtation will spare us the decision of whether or not we remain faithful to our spouse.

Jody couldn't deny that she was flattered when one of her coworkers began to flirt with her. Every morning she and Jim seemed to be in the cafeteria at the same time getting their coffee. Jim was light-hearted and energetic. He seemed to have a gift for making her laugh, and she found herself blushing at his obvious admiration.

There hadn't been many laughs recently in her six-year marriage. For that matter, there hadn't been much of anything. Brian's business was taking him out of town on a regular basis, and when he returned, he worked long hours to keep up with his workload. For months he had been preoccupied and remote. She hadn't realized how neglected she felt until Jim's flattering attention.

Jody was dimly aware that her prayer life had all but disappeared as her interest in Jim progressed. One morning on the way to work, she cautiously prayed for God to give her guidance. She had scarcely formulated the prayer when God seemed to say, "Jody, you already know my guidance!"

The rebuke was clear, and she had to admit to herself that she *did* indeed know what God had to say on the matter of shifting her attention away from her own husband.

There is no denying that it was difficult to give up the morning meetings that made her feel so special, but nonetheless she began taking her coffee back to her work area and avoiding the situation of being alone with Jim. A few weeks later, grateful relief accompanied her bruised pride when she observed how easily Jim turned his attentions to someone else.

Jody took the difficult step of telling her husband that she was feeling lonely and vulnerable. Brian immediately took measures to reduce his business travel, and, together, they began putting much-needed care and time into their marriage.

Her hesitant prayer and God's definite leading caused her to stop the office flirtation that could have eventually ruined her marriage.

Small decisions can reap large rewards and pay off in a life blessedly unmarred by upsets and trials. It's much easier to deal with marital problems as they arise than it is to repair broken trust, broken vows, and broken hearts.

PUT FIRST THINGS FIRST

In this book we have placed an emphasis on *seeking the counsel and experiences of other godly people* as valuable factors in learning to make wise decisions. While the Bible extols the virtues of godly counsel, it never suggests that it should take the place either of searching the Scriptures independently or seeking God's guidance in prayer.

But seek first his kingdom and his righteousness,
and all these things will be given to you as well. (Matt. 6:33)

Seeking out godly counsel should come *after* we have prayed about it and searched the Scriptures to discover God's Word on the matter. In the above verse the Lord has told us what our priority of action should be when we are confronted with a need—we are to seek him first.

Yet we often put the cart before the horse. As we hurry through our days, it's easier to pick up the phone, turn on the radio or television, or buy a book that seems to have done the seeking and the praying for us. As good as these resources are, if they are used exclusively, they can rob us of something very precious: relating personally to God.

Consider this hypothetical situation: Your company has offered you an enticing new position that would require moving the family to another state. If you rushed into the house and excitedly phoned a friend to help you sort out the pros and cons of the offer before discussing it with your spouse, it would be obvious that your priorities were out of order. The wisdom and input of others become valuable resources only when viewed in the larger context of your spouse's opinions and feelings. And so it is with the Lord. Until we have earnestly sought his guidance, there is no meaningful framework for making decisions. Nothing can substitute the diligent pursuit of God and his will through his Word.

> The tragedy
> of our day is not
> unanswered prayer
> but unoffered
> prayer.
> —UNKNOWN

Chuck and Lynn's decision to follow God's Word placed them in the uncomfortable position of choosing to disregard medical advice. Without the support of these experts, they relied on God and the support of other believers through a long and emotional trial.

When a prenatal ultrasound revealed a large tumor growing on the right side of their unborn baby's brain, Chuck and Lynn were speechless with grief. Four years earlier, their son was born with a rare form of hydrocephalus, and now their second baby had an even more rare condition.

The doctor presented a grim outlook—certain brain damage and possible blindness. There were only two options: continue the pregnancy and risk bringing this profoundly damaged life into the world or terminate the pregnancy and spare everyone years of pain and despair.

Chuck and Lynn's decision to continue the pregnancy seemed to baffle the doctor. To some, it may have seemed foolish and even reckless, but they relied on the counsel of a higher authority: the Word of

God. The Bible was clear that God knows each life even as it forms in the mother's womb. He regarded this precious little life as sacred.

Although the decision to continue the pregnancy was quickly made, the challenges continued. Several weeks later a second ultrasound was performed. Sadly, it only verified the presence of the tumor. Because of the rarity of the case, the doctor presented the ultrasounds to a convention of neuro-opthamologists. Chuck and Lynn's hope of any optimistic news vanished when the group agreed that the tumor would bring profound retardation and might even grow so rapidly to prevent a normal eye from developing.

During the long months of waiting, Chuck held on to a verse that he found one day during his Bible study. Jesus had come upon a man who had been born blind. The disciples asked Jesus if the blindness was the result of the man's sins or the sins of his parents. "'Neither this man nor his parents sinned,' said Jesus, 'but this happened so that the work of God might be displayed in his life'" (John 9:3). Jesus then went on to restore the blind man's sight. The Bible passage comforted Chuck and seemed to soothe the anger and guilt that plagued him.

The pregnancy progressed uneventfully to the ninth month. Labor started at 3:00 A.M. and by the time they arrived at the hospital, Lynn was almost ready to deliver. Less then two hours after her first contraction, Adam was born.

The doctor's eyes widened as he examined the baby. "Lynn, there's nothing there!" he shouted. "He looks normal!"

Chuck and Lynn were elated. After months of preparing themselves for the worst, they could barely comprehend the miracle that lay before them in the doctor's hands. A CAT scan confirmed that there was no evidence of a tumor.

The best evidence for this miracle has been Adam's healthy life. He's seventeen now—a senior in high school, a good student, and a varsity soccer player.

Looking back on it, Chuck and Lynn believe that God's will and purpose were in motion from the very beginning. Naturally, they were grateful beyond words for their healthy son, but they know they would have loved him regardless.

Trusting God was not the easy path, but their experience confirmed their belief that God is bigger than any circumstance.

If we really understood how much God loves us, we could also grasp how he longs for us to include him in every aspect of our lives. Martin Luther said, "Prayer is not overcoming God's reluctance, but laying hold of his willingness." Doesn't this sound like a God who purely delights in being involved in every aspect of our decision making?

THE PLACE OF GODLY COUNSEL

Sometimes we face decisions that are unusually complex and have the potential of bringing far-reaching consequences. These choices require special consideration, prayer, and often something else: wise counsel from other people.

Solomon, in the Book of Proverbs, had much to say about the wisdom of seeking wise counsel and advice:

Let the wise listen and add to their learning,
and let the discerning get guidance. (Prov. 1:5)
The way of a fool seems right to him,
but a wise man listens to advice. (12:15)
Plans fail for lack of counsel,
but with many advisers they succeed. (15:22)
Listen to advice and accept instruction,
and in the end you will be wise. (19:20)

Solomon praises the wisdom of listening. A foolish person thinks he knows it all, but a wise person is teachable and values the experiences of others. Implicit in these verses is the admonition to seek the counsel of the *wise*. Our counselors may have wisdom that came to them through their successes, their failures, or as a gift from God. The input of godly family and friends, of pastors and Christian counselors, can make the bumpy road of life immeasurably smoother. Our primary source, however, is the all-knowing counsel of God.

DECIDE TO DECIDE

Drive down most any residential street these days, and you will see homes with small signs near the front door indicating the house is wired with an alarm system. If a thief enters a home that is protected, a siren sounds and calls the police. People install alarm systems to protect their families and their possessions.

Sadly, some people take few precautions to protect their precious heart and soul. They leave the doors to their convictions and beliefs unguarded. Perhaps the desire to win the acceptance of society has become the most important goal. Jesus warned us that our strongest desires would rule our lives when he said, "For where your treasure is, there your heart will be also" (Matt. 6:21).

If we do not radiate the light of Christ around us, the sense of the darkness that prevails in the world will increase.
—MOTHER TERESA

Without a strong foundation of belief, compromised thinking can tiptoe in and steal the ability to discern truth from lies. One of the most seductive lies of our times is that all sincerely held beliefs are right—that all spiritual roads lead to heaven.

Most people would never believe such a sweeping generalization in other matters. If a salesman said that all cars, dishwashers, or cameras were equally good, potential buyers could pick out this scam in a heartbeat because they know there are countless differences in engineering, performance, safety, and reliability in almost every type of product.

If every religion or philosophy is accepted as truth, the essential message is that there is no absolute truth. This idea is greatly appealing to the masses because they are relieved of the responsibility of measuring their lives in view of an absolute moral yardstick. Ancient Israel experienced this absence of spiritual truth and leadership, and as a result, "everyone did what was right in his own eyes" (Judg. 21:25 NASB).

In contrast, Jesus warned us that his way would not be met with mass agreement or appeal.

> *"Enter through the narrow gate. For wide is the gate and*
> *broad is the road that leads to destruction, and many enter*
> *through it. But small is the gate and narrow the road that*
> *leads to life, and only a few find it." (Matt. 7:13–14)*

He further told us that while the gate is narrow it leads to a wide, liberating, and abundant life.

> *"I am the way and the truth and the life." (John 14:6)*

*"I have come that they may have life,
and have it to the full." (John 10:10b)
"Then you will know the truth,
and the truth will set you free." (John 8:32)*

In the world, there is huge competition for our hearts, minds, and souls, but settling for a comfortable and convenient "truth" leaves us exposed to every danger.

Brenda's open mind regarding spiritual matters led her to a path that promised peace but in reality delivered anxiety and hopelessness.

Brenda considered herself a "seeker." Her search started when she rejected the condemning and constraining views of the church in which she was raised. Along her road of discovery she had dabbled with transcendental meditation and humanistic self-help philosophies. But nothing seemed to ring true or provide a real basis for living life—much less answer her questions about what happened when this life ended.

After reading two books about astrology, she decided to have her astrological chart done for the year. She came into the session with many questions and decisions on her mind, but she left feeling that she had gotten more than she'd ever bargained for.

As Brenda sat expectantly across the table, the astrologer's expression reminded her of a doctor who was about to deliver a grim diagnosis to a patient. Brenda felt a chill as the woman unfolded predictions of a year beset with marital difficulties, financial struggles, and an "accident involving your child" sometime in late summer.

Brenda left the woman's home in near despair. What was she supposed to do with this information? Was her future cast in stone? Was there no hope? Rather than finding much-desired insight and understanding, she felt she had received a curse.

As she considered this depressing and hopeless experience, Brenda knew for certain that she would never again entrust herself to someone dealing in the occult. What good did it do to know the future if there was no caring presence there to guide and protect you?

Cautiously, Brenda began listening to Christian radio and television, where she heard about a God who was loving and caring. The Lord responded to her timid curiosity by slowly revealing himself as a God who cared about her personally. In Christ she found the compassion and love that she had been searching for all her life. Her decision to receive Christ ended her search through the dangerous quagmire of religions, philosophies, and the occult. Instead, she began a new life of peace and confidence.

Brenda's search for truth had a happy ending. Yet the seeking heart is a vulnerable heart, and God's guidance is never more essential. The Bible tells us, "If a blind man leads a blind man, both will fall into the pit" (Matt. 15:14). The way of the world would seem to cast a vast illumination on any number of ways to reach the truth, but in fact it leads only to a pit of lies. In stark contrast, God's light is a sharply focused beam that reveals only Jesus Christ.

> "I am the way and the truth and the life. No one comes to
> the Father except through me." (John 14:6)

God doesn't promise to cast before us the beam from a searchlight or a floodlight as we travel through life. He gives us a lamp—just enough light for each step.

> Your word is a lamp to my feet
> and a light for my path. (Ps. 119:105)

Through the pages of this book, you are invited to step inside the glow of the lamplight other people have experienced in their journey with God. By sharing their stories, we hope you will become more sensitive to God's leading and more confident in his love for you and his desire for your well-being.

THE MISSING PEACE

John and Emily met at a '50s party hosted by the church singles' group. The fellowship hall was virtually transformed into a malt shop that looked like it came straight from *Happy Days*. John wore blue jeans, a white T-shirt, and combed his dark hair into a slick ducktail. Emily was a vision in her saddle shoes, poodle skirt, and sweater set. Their attraction was immediate and mutual. They saw each other every day for the next month.

John was intense and quiet, but when he and Emily were alone, he opened up and relaxed. They took long walks, sipped cappuccinos, and contentedly watched television. They were falling in love. Five weeks after they met, John proposed marriage. Emily hesitated—they'd known each other for such a short time—but wasn't that the way fairy-tale romances went? She said yes.

Emily wanted a large, traditional wedding. John, however, insisted they keep it small and that they marry very soon. He really preferred an intimate ceremony—just the two of them before a justice of the peace.

Emily couldn't imagine being married anywhere other than the church, and her parents and friends had to share in such an important day. They fitfully agreed on a small church wedding to take place in two months. She was on cloud nine.

Her parents, however, didn't share her enthusiasm. "Honey," said her father, "you're normally so cautious and conservative." He laughed. "You've taken more time to pick out a dress!" His tone grew serious. "Are you sure about this?"

"Dad, I want you to meet him!" she answered. "Then you'll understand."

"Then why don't you come this weekend? We need to get to know the man who has captivated our daughter."

John and Emily made the trip, but when it was over, Emily knew that her parents still didn't know John. They tried, but John was so reserved that they just couldn't connect with him. Sometimes the tension was obvious, like one night when her dad asked John about his walk with the Lord. John visibly recoiled and answered sharply, "My faith is a private matter." Emily shuddered—was it normal for things to feel so awkward and uncomfortable?

The only time John was at ease was when he and Emily were alone. She tried to encourage him to open up, but he seemed perfectly content maintaining his distance.

He held her close. "Hey, I'm marrying you, not your family!"

A warning bell sounded in her head.

The following week her mom called. "Em, you know I wouldn't hurt you for the world, but I can't seem to shake these bad feelings I have about you and John marrying."

In spite of the warm spring evening, Emily felt a chill. "Oh, now, don't worry, Mom. And anyway, the invitations went out today. It's a done deal."

"No, Em. It's not a done deal until you say 'I do.' Remember that. Maybe you should consider postponing the wedding until you know each other better. If it's the real thing, he'll wait for you."

When they hung up, Emily tried not to feel angry. For heaven's sake, she was getting married! Was it too much to ask for her family to be happy for her? Didn't they know how hard it was to find a good man? Couldn't they just share in her joy?

Truth was, she hadn't been feeling much joy. Most of the time she felt worried or anxious. Maybe she just had a case of prewedding jitters. It didn't help that she and John seemed to be arguing more and more. When she mentioned this to him, he said, "If you had agreed to get married by a JP like I wanted, we'd be married now, and there would be nothing to fight about."

She was surprised by his angry sarcasm, but it encouraged her to speak her mind. "John, I've been thinking. Maybe we should go through the premarital counseling at church."

"No. No way! Either we're right for each other or we're not. I don't need a stranger's opinion on our relationship!" The door on the subject slammed shut.

Shortly after this, Emily told John she needed some time to catch up on her housework and call her girlfriends. She did neither. Instead, she spent the evening crying—and praying. "Lord, am I making a mistake? I thought this was the man you had for me, but I don't feel any peace. What should I do?"

There were no lightning bolts or instant answers. Just the memory of her mother's words: "If it's the real thing, he'll wait for you."

Emily called John the next day. "We need to talk. Can I come over?"

In his apartment Emily told him about her concerns. "This is the rest of our lives we're talking about, John. I think we need to postpone the wedding and get premarital counseling."

John seemed to change before her eyes. In his fury, he unleashed a barrage of insults and profanity. "I might have known you wouldn't have the guts to go against your parents—that's it, isn't it?"

She tried to reason with him, but it was of no use.

He held open the front door. "Get out of here! The wedding's off! We're off!"

Driving home, she felt as though she were in a dream. She never would have believed John capable of such cruelty and hate. Strangely, even through her tears, she found herself thanking God for making her uneasy about the marriage, for the wise counsel from her parents, for sparing her from what would have been a disastrous decision.

A couple of years later, Emily was engaged to marry Rob, a man she'd known for several years and had been dating for many months. This time, she wasn't looking for a fairy-tale experience but for the peace and certainty that comes from deep love and a wise, prayerful decision.

Today Emily and Rob have been married sixteen years. She's forever grateful for God's guidance that allowed her to feel the nagging emptiness of a wrong decision. When Rob came along, the difference was like night and day. He fit into her family like a missing puzzle piece. Circumstances may throw two people together, but when God brings a man and woman together, it's a match made in heaven.

THE NEW BUSINESS

"We are doing the right thing, aren't we?" asked Stephanie.

Matt answered, "Yes. I think so—I hope so!"

"Starting another business! Suddenly, I'm scared," said Stephanie.

Matt was too. Several years before, the combination of skyrocketing interest rates and the declining real estate market had dealt the final blows to their struggling contracting business. They did their best to save it, but eventually they sank to financial disaster. The stress and disappointment took a heavy toll. They were barely able to save their home; their marriage floundered. Memories of those awful, scary times rolled across their minds. Were they about to repeat the same mistakes, or were they stepping out in faith?

They tried to reassure themselves that this time was different. For several months Matt had been working out of the house, and business had steadily increased. He knew that in order to get new business he needed more space, more help, and additional equipment. They had found an affordable office and shop; they had a good contract and adequate start-up money since they'd taken out a loan on their house. Stephanie would keep the books and work in the office and still be home when the kids got in from school.

And there was another important difference. They had been praying together about their decisions—something that they rarely did before. Why, then, were they so scared? If God had led them here, shouldn't they feel peaceful and confident? Were the bad memories his way of warning them away from this venture?

The day was cold and gray, and the heat hadn't been turned on in the shop. As they huddled together, they discussed their options. They might be able to get out of their lease, but then what would they do? Contracting was what Matt knew, and he was good at it. Did one business failure mean they should never try again?

"Let's pray about it again, Steph." Matt took her hands. "Lord, we want to do what you want us to do. We thought this was where you were leading us. We've been praying about it for weeks. But suddenly it feels strange, and we have doubts. If you don't want us to start this business, that's okay; we'll walk away right now. But all we can do is go forward unless you make that clear to us. In Jesus' name, amen."

After dinner that night when the kids were busy with homework, Matt and Stephanie took a walk. Clouds blanketed the sky making the October evening feel milder and warmer than it had all day. Surprisingly, as they walked, they didn't talk about the new business at all. Matt seemed almost carefree. He chatted about a conversation he'd had with an old friend.

As Stephanie listened, she became aware of an unusual feeling of peace and well-being. Suddenly she was certain that the Lord was near—very near. She smiled into the darkness. He was walking with them, loving them, reassuring them. She felt overwhelmed by his radiant, peaceful presence.

She stopped, put her hand on Matt's arm and told him about it.

"We're going to be all right," she said. "As long as the Lord is our Partner, we don't have to be afraid of repeating past mistakes, because with him all things are made new."

Now, six years later, they can still recall the first day of their new business—the worry, the doubt, the fear—and God's gracious reminder that he is near. There have been many other decisions since then, and the usual ups, downs, and challenges of business. God has never revealed himself to them in quite the same way. But they learned that praying is only part of their partnership with God—the other part is listening. When pondering a decision, they still grab their sweaters and try to turn down the chatter in their minds by taking a walk. Whether they feel it or not, they know the Lord is walking with them.

A HOUSE UNITED

They were living in an old rental house in an industrial area when Brent came home one day excited about buying a lot in one of the most prestigious areas in the city. Lisa was taken off guard. They had only been married a few years, and now with a new baby, she was hoping that soon they could buy a "fixer-upper" and move their little family into a real neighborhood. Their contrasting expectations should have raised a red flag, but they approached this ominous crossroads with only casual caution.

In the realtor's plush car they drove to the foothills of the mountains. No one had to tell them they were in exclusive country. Adobe-style homes were tucked into the brush and jutted dramatically from the hillside.

Lisa wondered how a house could be built on rock and cliff. And even if there was a way, she had always pictured a traditional home set in the midst of a rolling lawn on a tree-lined street. There wasn't a conventional house or a blade of grass in sight.

Brent climbed on top of a huge boulder and pulled Lisa beside him. "Just look at the view."

The sun was setting in a brilliant display of pinks, corals, and blues. The city sprawled at their feet like an Indian rug.

"Yes," she said. "It is a beautiful view."

From the corner of her eye, she caught the flash of a smile between Brent and the realtor.

They bought the lot. With the large land payment, their budget was stretched to the max. It was another three years before they were able to buy a small house. It was far from perfect, they agreed. The schools weren't the best, and the neighborhood didn't have many kids. The bedrooms were small and there was only one bathroom, but if everything worked out, they'd only be there a year or two.

Ten years later Lisa was growing increasingly restless and frustrated with their small home. With four of them now, they staggered their bath schedule, but other problems like the poor schools were not so easily solved. More and more frequently Lisa brought up the subject of moving, and more and more frequently, they argued.

"Let's sell the land and buy a bigger house in a better neighborhood," she urged.

Brent countered, "I don't want to give up my dream of having a house on the land."

"But we can't afford to build up there!"

"Then we'll just have to wait."

"For how long?" she shouted. "Until the kids are grown? You're the only one who wants to live there anyway. I've never even liked the land!"

There it was—the root of their problem laid bare. Just as on that very first day, they were still at odds on the land. Lisa had gone along with buying the lot to avoid conflict, but it had only postponed and prolonged it, creating an even deeper division between them.

One day after an all-too-frequent argument, Brent said, "Let's just sell it and buy another house; it's not worth us fighting all the time."

She knew his heart wasn't really in it, but Lisa set out the next day, checking out neighborhoods, writing down addresses of homes she liked, and phoning realtors. However, when she took Brent to see the houses, there was no end to his objections: "It's too uninteresting," or "it's so old it'll cost a fortune to fix up." Or, "It's too new. There are no trees." Or, "There's no view." Something every time.

Discouragement was setting in. Brent didn't seem to care whether they found a house or not. Deep down they knew they were as divided as ever.

Brent came home from work one day and said, "I talked to the accountant today about buying a house. He said it would be best if we could find someone who wanted to trade for the land."

Lisa exploded. "You can't be serious! What are the odds of finding a house we both like that's owned by someone who just happens to want to trade for the land? We can't agree on a house even without that factor!"

Brent just shrugged and walked away.

In the kitchen Lisa wept and prayed. "Lord, if you want us to move, you're going to have to show us how and where. I'm afraid this problem is going to ruin our marriage! Please show us what *you* want for us."

It was not the first time she'd prayed about the house conflict, but it was the first time she had stopped imposing her own solutions upon God. She felt the relief of setting down a heavy load.

A few days later Brent came home unexpectedly for lunch. While they were eating, the phone rang. It was a builder friend of theirs that Lisa had spoken with a month or two earlier.

"Say," he said, "it just occurred to me that I have a house you and Brent might like." He went on, "I have a client who's interested in your land—maybe we could work out some kind of trade."

Lisa could scarcely believe her ears. "A trade? What's the house like?"

"Well, it's kind of an unusual house. It's been remodeled recently. It has a view of the mountains, three bedrooms . . . ."

She held her hand over the phone to tell Brent.

"Ask him how many bathrooms."

Lisa held her breath as she listened. She smiled at Brent. "Two and a half . . . ."

"Tell him we'll be right over."

To this day, Lisa and Brent are amazed at God's creativity in bringing them to a home that blended their individual preferences yet uniquely reflected them as a couple.

The Bible says that a house divided against itself shall not stand. Brent and Lisa learned this lesson the long, hard way. They know that had God not intervened their division might have torn them apart.

As a result of their experience, they have dramatically changed their decision-making process. No longer do they choose to avoid a momentary conflict at the expense of being truly united on important decisions. They start early praying about a decision, and sometimes they sit down and write down the pros and cons of an issue so they can understand it more clearly. When one of them is strongly opposed to something, the issue is tabled until there is real agreement or a workable compromise.

They know that even cherished dreams can become nightmares if they lose sight of God and each other in their pursuit. It took the Lord to teach them that and to create a house united.

— —

Looking Back on Lessons Learned

- If making decisions seems to be a random, haphazard process, we need to realign ourselves in our daily walk with the Lord.
- A very wise request is to ask God for wisdom.
- By looking squarely at our failures, we can learn from them, and with God's help, we can avoid repeating them.
- If we are involved in blatant sin, God may be silent in response to our prayers. Once we have obediently dealt with the sin by taking the action we already know to be right, we will find that our communion with the Lord has opened up.
- Small, good decisions will help create a life free of upsets and crises.
- If we want wise advice, we must consult wise people.
- When conventional wisdom contradicts God's Word, follow God's Word.
- Our strongest desires will dictate the course of our lives. As Jesus told us, "For where your treasure is, there your heart will be also" (Matt. 6:21).
- We should not allow ourselves to be rushed into important decisions. Wait until the decision brings a sense of peace.
- Choosing the "narrow" way of Jesus doesn't mean leading a narrow life. On the contrary, Jesus said that he came so that we might have life to the full.
- The Lord can move us away from harmful actions or decisions by blocked opportunities, the counsel of wise relatives and friends, or our own lack of peace.
- Praying for guidance is only part of the process. The other part is listening for God's response.

2

Success Is a Journey, Not a Destination

Most people equate success with wealth, power, and happiness. But true success is not a thing you acquire or achieve. Rather, it is a journey you take your whole life long.
JOHN C. MAXWELL

Word that Stewart Adams was dying spread quickly throughout the small community. A stream of friends and family filed in to his hospital room to say their good-byes to the soft-spoken old gentleman. Doctors and nurses watched in wonder as the waiting room filled with people from all walks of life. Mr. Adams appeared to be just another elderly patient whose life was drawing to a close, yet it was obvious that he had touched many people.

At first look, there was nothing remarkable about Mr. Adam's life. He was neither rich nor well educated, and his only property was the small frame house where he and his wife, Nona, had raised their family of five children.

For thirty-five years Stewart worked in a tile manufacturing plant where he eventually became the shift supervisor. He took his work to heart and was respected for his fair but high expectations of his crew. He was not a prideful man, but the fact that he had never missed a day of work was a private source of satisfaction.

Even through hard times, Stewart Adams managed to provide for his family. There was never an abundance of money in the bank, but the family was always fed, the tithe faithfully dropped into the collection plate, and the bills paid. When a friend was in need, Stewart would quietly press a few dollars into his palm as they shook hands to say farewell.

Through lean months he sometimes couldn't figure out how the money had lasted. In spite of this, when four of his five children wanted to go college, he and Nona sacrificed and saw to it that they went. With only an eighth-grade education himself and less than that for Nona, they stood tall, eyes bright with emotion, as all four of those children graduated from college.

Both Stewart and Nona were devoted to their church. Nona must have cooked for hundreds of potlucks and taken dishes to countless people down with sickness or new babies. Stewart found his niche teaching Sunday school. As the years progressed, he came to be thought of as the church's resident grandpa. Children vied for the coveted spot on his lap as, from memory, he told them stories from the Bible. His faith was as straightforward and as honest as his life. He read the Bible every day, believed it, and did his best to live it.

Stewart and Nona seemed as constant as the sunrise, but Stewart's life grew dark when, after fifty-three years of marriage, Nona died. His children were at his side, and his oldest daughter begged him to come live with her family in Atlanta. Stewart kissed her cheek. "No, thank you, sweetheart. The good Lord planted me here, and I'll stay here until he calls me home."

Mr. Adams left the earth without an impressive estate to show for his life; but he left a rich legacy of a life lived in integrity, humility, and love.

By worldly standards, Stewart Adams would not be considered successful. He didn't own a fine home, drive a new car, or have a comfortable nest egg. Yet he lived a life filled with meaning and satisfaction. He possessed what can never be purchased but is highly prized: peace. It's easy to imagine his arrival in heaven. There was probably a celebration and a joyful reunion with Nona, and then the precious words of the Savior, "Well done, good and faithful servant!"

WHAT IS TRUE SUCCESS?

Webster defines *success* as "obtaining a favorable or desired outcome." This definition stops short of addressing the issue of *how* the favored or desired outcome was achieved. Therefore, the college student who desires an "A" on an algebra test and gets it is successful.

But what if she got her "A" by cheating? Is she still a success? A man might have set his sights on becoming vice president of the company, but what if he ruthlessly used people and lied his way into the coveted corner office? He might have succeeded in reaching his goal, but his methods were successful only in eroding his character. It is clear that success is more than just reaching the destination; it's the journey there as well.

> *Prefer a loss to a dishonest gain; the one brings pain at the moment, the other for all time.*
> —CHILTON

We tend to think of "success" in the context of big, stand-up-and-take-notice accomplishments, but it's far more than that. Every accomplishment, no matter how small, is a success if it honors God.

> *And whatever you do, whether in word or deed, do it all*
> *in the name of the Lord Jesus, giving thanks to God the*
> *Father through him. (Col. 3:17)*

From God's perspective a simple word of encouragement to a hurting friend or a trying day spent wiping the runny nose of a cranky two-year-old is a success if we have done it in love to his glory.

There will be the occasional and thrilling pinnacle moments when we receive the degree or get the raise, but true success is measured as much by the little things we accomplish each day as it is by the big things we achieve over a lifetime. Failing to acknowledge the small, seemingly insignificant successes robs us of the daily joys of godly living.

WHAT'S YOUR PURPOSE?

"What is your purpose in life?" The two most common responses given to this question are "I don't know" and, "I'm not sure." It is estimated that only 20 percent of the adult American population can verbalize what they perceive to be their purpose in life.

At the heart of every good work or accomplishment is purpose. Mother Teresa's purpose was to serve the poor. Martin Luther King Jr. worked to promote racial equality. The apostles' purpose was to share the good news of Jesus Christ. As a lighthouse beacon guides a ship safely into the harbor, a clear purpose in life guides our thoughts and actions toward our goals. By fulfilling our purpose, we experience the joy and satisfaction of a meaningful life.

Ever since missionaries visited his church when he was ten years old, John knew he wanted to tell people about Jesus Christ. Following high school, he entered the Air Force Academy, where he began his training as a fighter pilot. For fifteen years he proudly served his country while sharing the gospel with anyone who expressed an interest.

Years later, after retiring from the military, John was offered a position flying for a large commercial airline. Although he was tempted, John turned down the lucrative job. Instead, he accepted an offer to fly missionaries in and out of remote areas of the African jungle. It was a risky endeavor, but John knew it was the fulfillment of a dream that started when he was ten years old.

When we know our purpose in life, we have a huge advantage in the decision-making process. John wanted to be involved in bringing people to Christ, so when the opportunity came to bring Christ to the people, he was confident that he had found the way to fulfill his dream.

> For we are God's workmanship, created in Christ Jesus
> to do good works, which God prepared in advance
> for us to do. (Eph. 2:10)

Christians have a distinct advantage when it comes to determining our purpose. The elements of a successful and purposeful life were revealed when Jesus told us the "greatest commandment."

> "'Love the Lord your God with all your heart and with all
> your soul and with all your mind.' . . . 'Love your neighbor
> as yourself.'" (Matt. 22:37, 39)

This is a liberating command that can take myriad forms. As we discern, with God's leading, how to use our gifts, talents, and interests to love God and love others, the specifics of our calling become as individual as we are.

If we are still struggling to find our niche, it's never too late for prayer, wise counsel, and an honest examination of our individual desires and abilities. Not everyone is cut out to be a missionary. You may discover that your purpose is to raise and nurture your children, provide sustenance for your family, serve in government, teach, or be involved in medical research. God is a big God, and he is able to bless us and use us wherever we are if our hearts and minds are fixed on him.

THE MYTH OF SMOOTH SAILING

It would be great if, after determining our purpose in life, we sailed over calm waters to our destination. Unfortunately, the seas are often rough and we can be tossed around and thrown off course. In such cases, it's tempting to think that we have failed and will never be useful to God again.

Discouragement is one of Satan's favorite and most effective weapons. It can deflate us so we let circumstances, feelings, or other people control our future. Elaine, in the following story, fell prey to disappointment and bitterness.

Elaine was fifty years old, but she looked seventy. For fifteen alcohol-blurred years, she had been in and out

You always pass failure on the way to success.
—UNKNOWN

of destructive relationships, shabby apartments, and homeless shelters. Her shoulders slumped in defeat as she shuffled along with eyes downcast.

Elaine had known a better life. She was born in upstate New York to a well-to-do family who gave her every advantage. She went to college and got her degree, but in her heart all she really wanted was to be married and raise a family. When she met Stan, she thought her dreams had come true.

For a few years all seemed to be well between them. But when Elaine began talking about starting their family, Stan grew edgy and distant. One evening, Elaine came home to a letter left on the kitchen table. In stunned silence, she read that Stan no longer wanted the responsibility of a wife and certainly not of children. For months, he had been secretly involved with another woman, and he now wanted to end their marriage.

Elaine was overwhelmed with feelings of failure and rejection. Brokenhearted, she blamed Stan for ruining her dream of having children and a family. Over the next several years, she bounded from one disastrous choice to another. Each time she found herself in a mess, her anger burned toward Stan. In her eyes, he was the cause of every problem she had.

More and more frequently, she drank herself into a numbing stupor. Her parents tried to help, but eventually they stopped giving her money that would only be spent in the liquor store. In anger, Elaine vowed never to see them again.

At age fifty, Elaine was a solitary, homeless alcoholic. Fifteen years after finding the letter on the kitchen table, she was still quick to say that Stan had ruined her life.

The average person is unlikely to end up living on the streets because of a broken heart. Many people, however, lose a little hope when they are dealt a difficult blow, and they quietly wonder if anything good will come from their lives again.

It is painful to experience brokenness in our lives; however, God can take every hurt and disappointment and cause them to yield beautiful results.

> *He has sent me to bind up the brokenhearted, to proclaim*
> *freedom for the captives and release from darkness for the*
> *prisoners, . . . to comfort all who mourn, and provide for those*
> *who grieve in Zion—to bestow on them a crown of beauty*
> *instead of ashes, the oil of gladness instead of mourning, and*
> *a garment of praise instead of a spirit of despair. (Isa. 61:1–3)*

Both our successes and our setbacks help make us the person we are. When we walk with God through our pain, we grow closer to him and more compassionate toward others who have also suffered. Elaine's feelings of rejection and failure consumed her, and eventually this outlook gained control of her life. Although her heartbreak and hurt were justified, it was her own bitterness that ruined her life.

THE SECRET OF TRUE SUCCESS

There is a secret ingredient to living a successful life: obedience to God. The decision to obey God is one we must make constantly throughout the course of our lifetime. The Old Testament gives us a prime illustration of this in the life of King Uzziah. At the age of sixteen, Uzziah was crowned king of Jerusalem, over which he ruled for fifty-two years.

He began his reign wisely by seeking out godly counsel from the prophet Zechariah. The prophet instructed him to be obedient to God and seek his guidance in all things. King Uzziah made the choice to obey God and follow his commands, and he was successful. "As long as he sought the Lord, God gave him success" (2 Chron. 26:5).

Using this formula for success, King Uzziah was a powerful man who accomplished great things. Unfortunately, at the height of his power, Uzziah lost sight of the source of his good fortune, and he began to be prideful and unfaithful to God. He believed that he was so great and deserving of honor that he no longer needed the consecrated priests to burn incense in the sanctuary—he would do it himself. This action led to his political downfall, God's punishment, and his eventual death. "But after Uzziah became powerful, his pride led to his downfall" (2 Chron. 26:16).

> *God's mark is on everything that obeys him.*
> —MARTIN LUTHER

If we have experienced some degree of success, it can be tempting to believe that our own hard work, intelligence, and ability are solely responsible. It's only a short step from there to believing we are better than other people are. Proverbs 16:18 reinforces the principle that was at work in the life of King Uzziah: "Pride goes before destruction, a haughty spirit before a fall." Pride is literally the oldest sin in the book. Satan exalted himself and wanted to make himself "like the Most High" (see Isa. 14:14). Today the results of pride are still the same: separation from God.

Thinking that our success makes us special or deserving of unique privileges puts us in a prime position for failure and disappointment. If success causes us to boast or become anything other than a humble and obedient servant of God, it would be better never to have experienced it (see Phil. 2:3-8).

> This is what the LORD says:
> "Let not the wise man boast of his wisdom
> or the strong man boast of his strength
> or the rich man boast of his riches,

> but let him who boasts boast about this:
> that he understands and knows me,
> that I am the LORD, who exercises kindness,
> justice and righteousness on earth,
> for in these I delight," declares the LORD. (Jer. 9:23–24)

For the believer, the basis of true success is our walk with Christ because it influences and supports every aspect of our lives. When our lives are based on faith in God, we will succeed in the truly important matters. We can count on the fact that worldly values will ultimately fail us and disappoint us.

When death comes knocking at our own door, the house, the car, and the corner office will hardly matter. But if we can confidently echo the words of the apostle Paul, "I have fought the good fight, I have finished the race, I have kept the faith" (2 Tim. 4:7), we will have lived a successful life.

EATING HIS HEART OUT

The grandfather clock in the hall was striking 1:00 A.M. when Albert tiptoed down the stairs to the kitchen. He couldn't sleep. Scenes from the previous day played like an endless rerun through his mind. He saw himself running the track in gym class. His classmates had long ago headed to the showers, but Albert's weight had ensured that once again he would be the last one back to the locker room.

A group of senior kids sat on the bleachers and watched the spectacle of Albert, fifty pounds overweight, running the last lap.

"Hey, Hey, Hey!" they chanted, "Here comes fat Albert!"

Albert grabbed his gear, smiled, and lifted his water bottle to the group in a toast. They collapsed in laughter.

Standing in the kitchen, Albert shook his head and tried to clear the humiliating scene from his mind. The freezer emitted a blast of cold air that caused a deep shiver to travel through his body to his toes. He pulled out a bag of frozen doughnuts and put several of them on a paper towel. A creaking sound from upstairs caused him to quickly wrap the doughnuts in the paper towel and place them in the trash. He stood at the foot of the stairs listening. *Good. No one was up.*

Back in the kitchen he retrieved the doughnuts from the trash. He couldn't risk waiting for them to thaw. He shifted his weight from one foot to the other on the cold linoleum floor and ate the frozen dough-nuts while tears ran down his cheeks.

How he wished he could turn to his parents! But instead of help-ing him with this problem, his father never missed an opportunity to berate him. "Use some will power, for crying out loud!" He looked Albert up and down, assessing him in disgust. "I could never let myself reach such a revolting weight. I sometimes wonder if you're really my son."

When Albert looked to his mother for support and compassion, she sadly glanced away and said nothing.

It wasn't as though he hadn't tried to lose weight. There wasn't a diet he hadn't been on. He had eaten countless grapefruits, eggs, and celery sticks. He had weighed and measured his food; he had kept diaries, taken pills, and exercised to exhaustion. It was always the same—he'd lose for awhile and then something upsetting would hap-pen in his life, and he would turn to food. With each diet he grew more discouraged, more convinced that he had no value, and more overweight. And with every failure, his father was there to confirm his utter worthlessness.

Years later when he was grown, Albert could still clearly recall the despair of that time and his deep self-hatred. Although he had mar-ried and made a life for himself, his overweight and the sadness and anger of his childhood were still his constant companions. His wife accepted him and loved him as he was, but she knew that deep inside he remained broken and hurting.

One night Albert and his wife went to a movie with Albert's par-ents. Afterwards, they decided to stop for a cup of coffee. As they stepped into the restaurant an enormously overweight man squeezed by them as he exited the restaurant through the narrow doorway.

Albert's dad was clearly appalled. He turned to Albert and said, "That will be you if you don't stop eating so much!"

Albert was stunned and tension filled the air. His dad usually con-fined his put-downs to times when they were alone. After they were seated, his father, perhaps sensing that he had gone too far, tried to turn the conversation to other topics. All his life, Albert had avoided confronting his dad about his rejecting remarks and his constant crit-icisms. But that was about to end. As uncomfortable as it was for everyone, right then and there, he finally told his dad how his verbal abuse had caused him to suffer and feel worthless for much of his life.

"Dad, the only time you've ever told me you were proud of me was when I graduated from college."

To Albert's amazement, his father seemed genuinely unaware of the impact of his words and actions. After an initial wave of defensive excuses, for the first time in Albert's life, his father apologized to him. "I'm sorry, son. I promise, I'll never say another word about your weight." The confrontation and the long-awaited apology broke through an invisible wall in Albert's heart.

For as long as he could remember, Albert had prayed that God would show him how to control his weight. When he heard about a Christian program designed to help believers deal with emotional eating, he was skeptical, but he asked his wife to buy it for him for his birthday.

Through the program, Albert was able to see that his desire to please other people had taken him in the opposite direction of peace and fulfillment. He learned that living a healthy life meant being honest in his relationships and being willing to endure the short-term pain of handling a problem for the sake of the long-term good.

Most importantly, Albert realized he had always held back in his relationship with God. Perhaps he felt that God might reject him as his own father had. Whatever the reason, he was now willing to confront his fears of failure and unreservedly trust in the Lord. To him, that meant filling himself with the Holy Spirit through the Word of God rather than trying to find contentment through food. Within weeks the pounds began to come off. Several months later he had dropped an astonishing sixty-five pounds.

Reaching his life-long goal of losing weight was not so much a matter of personal will power as it was placing his trust in God's power and God's proven love. "Today, I'm less concerned about what others think of me, yet my relationships are stronger," said Albert. "My goal is to please God in the way I live my life. My true worth comes from him, and as long as I keep my eyes on him, I know I'll be okay."

She was standing at the sink scrubbing the broiler when Paul came up behind her and wrapped his arms around her. "Rosie, why don't you let that soak so we can take a late-night walk?"

She looked over her shoulder at him. "Paul, it's almost bedtime! And anyway, I've got to clean the oven and bleach the grape juice stains off the floor before they set."

"The moon is so bright, it's almost like daylight," said Paul, enticing her. "How about if I pitch in and clean the oven while you do the floor? We'll have it done in no time."

Rose gave him a weak smile. "You know I like it done a certain way. Anyway, it's too late for a walk."

There was an awkward silence. "But—thanks anyway, honey."

Paul nodded. Yes, after twenty years of marriage, he knew that Rose liked things done a certain way—perfectly, and at a certain time—constantly. He kissed her on the cheek. "Well, goodnight, Rosie. I'm going to read to the kids and go on to bed. See you in the morning."

He sounded understanding, but Rose saw the sadness in his eyes, and this caused her momentarily to stop her scrubbing. *Doesn't he appreciate our clean home?* She thought. *His house is always clean, the laundry is always done, and the kids are always neat—most men would appreciate that!* But Rose knew what Paul would say—it was what he'd said so many times before: "Relax, Rosie! The house is just a house! The kids and I want you, not a perfect house!"

Easy enough to say! thought Rose. *I wonder if he'd feel the same if I really did stop taking care of things? He gets to be the sentimental, easygoing father because I'm taking care of everything else!*

In truth, Rose knew that Paul usually offered to help, but when he did, she always had to clean it over—he never did a very thorough job. The boys did a few chores around the house, but it seemed that lately they just tried to avoid Rose and avoid being at home. The other day she overheard nine-year-old Jeffrey on the phone with one of his friends. "Nah," he'd said. "We'd better not play over here. My mom doesn't like us to mess up the house. I'll come over there."

Tears stung Rose's eyes. All she had ever wanted was to be a good homemaker. Yet it seemed that the nicer she kept things, the more she was criticized. Was this what she got in return for her efforts—an ungrateful family?

Saturday morning Paul suggested they go out to lunch and take in a matinee, but Rose decided against it.

"I'm in the middle of reorganizing the backyard storage shed and everything's a mess," she said. "I want to get it finished today. You go on by yourself."

Paul was irritated. "I don't want to go by myself, Rose. I want to go with you!"

"Then you'll just have to wait until I'm done," she said firmly.

In the storage shed Rose replayed the conversation. Sometimes Paul got so upset and emotional over a little thing like not going to a movie. He just hadn't been raised with the strong work ethic like she had. Her father's words still rang in her ears: "Work before play!" he had always said.

A sharp pain in her left shoulder blade caused Rose to sit down on a wooden crate. *I must have pulled a muscle,* she thought. She rubbed her shoulder and got back to work, but the pain came again. Stronger this time, it took her breath away. It traveled down her arm and spread across her chest. It felt like someone was sitting on her. She heard the screen door slam.

"Paul!" she called.

It was the last thing she remembered.

Rose opened her eyes in a hospital room; Paul stood at her side. "Hi, Rosie. I thought I'd lost you."

It was a shock to learn that at age forty-two, she'd had a massive heart attack and needed triple bypass surgery. She was slightly over-weight, but the doctors felt that her constant stress was probably the root of the problem.

After the surgery the doctor put it bluntly, "Rose, your family tells me you're a perfectionist. Either you are going to have to give up the idea that everything has to be perfect, or you're going to be perfectly dead."

As plain as that was, Rose still initially struggled with letting go of her demanding standards. After much prayer and conversation with

Paul, she discovered that she had really been striving for more than a perfectly clean and neat home. She had been measuring her self-worth and success by the way her home and family appeared. From the unique perspective brought about by facing death, she could finally see what a rigid and false yardstick that had been. She had been missing out on all the truly important things in life that were easily within her reach, but she had somehow failed to grasp. It was as if she had been surrounded with riches while living in self-imposed poverty. As Rose began to understand how her perfectionism had robbed herself and her family of joy, it was difficult not to replace her perfectionism with self-condemnation.

Time helped. Through the months of healing, the family spent hours together playing board games, working jigsaw puzzles, watching videos, and popping popcorn. Rose laughed with delight when her sons did impressions and told her jokes, and she cried with joy as they stooped to kiss her cheek each night before they went to bed.

Paul, as ever, was her rock. She marveled at his patience as she learned to express her affection for him and give him the attention that he deserved. She had been on the sidelines of her own life, but now the formerly detached and unemotional Rose was finally allowing herself to get into the messy, magical game of life and love.

"Hey, Rosie, it's a beautiful sunset. Let's take a walk."

Rose was slicing carrots for a salad. He came up behind her and wrapped his arms around her as he presented her with a pink rose.

"Oh, Paul, it's just beautiful."

"A perfect rose for my perfect Rosie," he said.

She smiled at him. "No. Not even close, and proud of it!"

RECYCLED ANGELS

Santiago sat in the hot tub in his backyard. The pulsing water provided only the slightest temporary relief from his unrelenting pain. The lights went on in the kitchen, and he watched Jolene as she moved around the room preparing dinner. She was the constant in his life—unchanging and supportive through his unimaginable succession of health problems.

A wave of despair fell over him. "God," he prayed. "I guess you aren't going to let me die right away, although I sometimes wish you would. What kind of an existence can I have now? What do you want me to do?"

Until five years ago he felt his life was an obvious success. He and Jolene and their son, Santi, bicycled, hiked, skied, motorcycled, fished, bowled, and played basketball—anything and everything athletic. As much as he loved his active leisure activities, they paled in comparison to his love for his work as a special education teacher. It was such a part of him that he used to say, "It's not what I do, it's what I am."

Even his work as a teacher was intensely active and physical. Unfortunately, his problems had started on a snowy day when he slipped on the ice in the school parking lot and landed on his back. At the time, he had no idea how serious his injuries were. After a few months of trying to deal with the pain, he had his first surgery to fuse two herniated disks. Even after the painful surgery and long recovery, the relief proved to be short-lived. In the year that followed, he would need three additional back surgeries—the final one kept him out of work for a year and a half and left him with a permanent limp. The doctor said a knee-replacement surgery would be essential, but he wasn't strong enough at the time to go through it.

Finally he was able to return to teaching. He had hoped that he would continue getting stronger and eventually resume a normal life. But those dreams came to an end one day while working with a group of twelve high school kids in his special education class.

The kids were in the school swimming pool, and Santiago was concentrating his efforts on a girl with epilepsy. Suddenly, she began flailing as she was being overtaken by a seizure. Santiago immediately grabbed her and swam her to the edge of the pool. He climbed out and then stooped to lift her from the pool, but as he pulled her up, he felt a sickening "pop" in his back. The pain was immediate, but he continued holding her as she seizured so that his body would take the brunt of the powerful gyrations. Ironically, after the frightening episode, she was fine, but Santiago was left in agonizing pain. He was in bed for the next two weeks.

Not long after this, the doctor told Santiago that he couldn't wait any longer for his knee replacement. He felt it would be a relatively simple procedure and a three-day hospital stay. However, after the surgery Santiago's lungs unexpectedly began filling with fluid and his kidneys started to fail. He somehow managed to pull through. Thankfully, his kidneys were undamaged, but his recovery took much longer than anticipated.

By this time, Santiago had missed so much work that he was advised to retire. He was only fifty-five. He had pictured many more years working with his special kids followed by a real retirement when he and Jolene could travel and pursue the activities they enjoyed. He felt discarded and useless with nothing to look forward to.

These were his feelings as he prayed in the hot tub that evening. There had once been a time when he felt he could successfully accomplish whatever he set his mind to. Now he was practically an invalid. He realized he had absolutely nothing to offer God but his meager faith. "I'm turning my life over to you, Lord. You just do whatever you want with it."

A few evenings later Santiago grabbed a can of pop from the refrigerator and went out to the backyard. He positioned his chair so he could watch the sunset turn the mountains a glowing watermelon pink before the sky grew dark.

Jolene was in the kitchen, and the light from the window streamed into the yard. As he lifted the soft drink can to his mouth, the light glimmered off the top of it, and what Santiago saw in that instant stopped his arm in midair. An angel! He could see the outline of a perfect little angel on the top of the can! Was he going completely nuts? Were his medications playing tricks on him?

"Jolene!" he called. "Come out here and bring the kitchen scissors!"

As Santiago snipped the top of the can, Jolene watched with furrowed brow. "An angel? Are you sure? I just don't see it."

But when he finished cutting, there it was—a tiny tin angel. Over the next days and weeks, Santiago used tin snips and leather working tools and began fashioning a variety of angels out of the lids of tin cans. Jolene contributed her artistic talents by painting delicate baskets of flowers or simple wildflowers on their skirts. There seemed to be no end to their ideas and designs. They made pins, wind chimes, wreaths, and wall hangings.

When Santi came home from college and saw what his dad was doing, Santiago braced himself to be teased. Instead, his son said,

"Dad, these are great. You ought to start selling them. I think people would really like them."

Santiago has made eight hundred different sizes, colors, and styles of angels. He sells them at crafts shows, gift and florist shops, and specialty "Angel" stores. When he sells at crafts fairs, he is often blessed with the privilege of hearing people talk about their personal experiences with God's real angels. Sometimes he even picks up some good ideas. One woman asked if he would make four angels for her and print the words *hope, love, peace,* and *faith* on each one.

Later, as he made her angels, it occurred to him to begin praying over each angel he made. He would send it out into the world with the hope that it would bring God's love, faith, and peace to whoever received it.

Santiago marvels that his "Recycled Angels" have been such a success. He once thought success depended on being strong and capable, but God changed that notion. He knows now that being a success means honoring God by doing what he can with what he has. It was a lesson that brought him new purpose and joy at a time when he thought his life was as useless as an empty tin can.

LOOKING BACK ON LESSONS LEARNED

- The best and most important things in life are not acquired with money but by the investments of our time, our love, and ourselves.
- Living a life defined by integrity, humility, and servanthood will result in a life that honors God.
- Wise decisions are often a by-product of a clearly defined purpose in life.
- God can use our hurts, disappointments, and failures as stepping-stones to our future success.
- The little things we do every day measure our success as surely as the big things we achieve over a lifetime.
- Our success in life is in direct proportion to our obedience to God.
- If our goal is to win the acceptance and approval of others, we will ultimately feel disappointed and empty. In fact, we would worry a lot less about what others think about us if we realized just how little they do.

- Mutual relationships based upon open, honest, and direct communication will bring the greatest rewards.
- Finding the right balance between work and leisure will spare us countless problems and lead to a more satisfying life.
- True self-worth comes with knowing who we are in Christ.
- God's will for our lives becomes most evident when we reach the point of surrendering our will to his.
- Each person has at least one God-given gift or talent. The degree to which we choose to use our gift for his glory is the degree to which we will experience true fulfillment.
- One of the greatest sources of satisfaction is simply spending time with those we care about and love.
- When all is said and done, our life will not be measured by what we have done but by the people we have touched.

3
—

Planting Seeds in Your Field of Dreams

*If one advances confidently in the direction of his
dreams, and endeavors to live the life which he has imagined,
he will meet with a success unexpected in common hours.*
HENRY DAVID THOREAU

*D*reamers are both reviled and revered in our culture. We love to
rally behind the dreamer and cheer him to victory. If he hopes to
sail around the world, we wish him fair weather; if he wants to write
a novel, we envision a best-seller; if he dreams of leaving the corpo-
rate job to strike out on his own, we hope for success. The old saying
is true: "All the world loves a dreamer." There comes a time, however,
when talk needs the support of action. If talking about the dream
becomes more appealing than pursuing the dream, both the dreamer
and his supporters will grow frustrated and weary. Proverbs 14:23
puts it in a nutshell: "All hard work brings a profit, but mere talk leads
only to poverty."

WAKING UP TO REALITY

One of the most common regrets expressed by people at the end
of life is having not pursued their dreams. Unfortunately, it's a rare
individual who sees his dream become reality. Most of us go to our
jobs, pick up the kids, grocery shop, and clean the house while our
dreams languish in the land of "someday." It's easy to allow life to simply happen to us rather than actively and strategically planning our
course.

Maybe we fail to dignify our dreams with actions because we
don't give our dreams the respect they deserve. The mere word *dream*

conjures up images of vague, gauzy shapes set in bizarre circumstances. But, in truth, our dreams are often where our purpose in life finds our unique expression. For instance, if you feel that your purpose is to help underprivileged children, then your dream of starting a summer camp in the country becomes a significant step toward achieving both your dream and your life purpose.

When we stop dreaming dreams and start planning goals, we have given our desires shape and definition. This is an important step toward making our dreams come true. A *goal* is just a dream that has woken up to reality. Despite the demands of life that compel us to give our time and attention to the practical and functional, is there a realistic way to pursue our dreams?

IF YOU SET THEM, THEY WILL COME

Setting goals allows us to plan where we want to go in life. In the process we determine what is important, and, as a result, we are more inclined to let go of activities that are distractions. Goal setting gives us long-term vision and short-term motivation—a rich return on our efforts. In addition, people who set goals typically suffer less stress and anxiety and have higher concentration and self-confidence. Regardless of our background, education, or past failures, setting God-honoring goals improves our quality of life.

> *The world stands aside to let anyone pass who knows where he is going.*
> —DAVID STARR JORDAN

Making sure that our goals honor God is central to our success. This concept is dramatically illustrated through the life of Nehemiah. As cupbearer to King Artaxerxes in Persia in 444 B.C., Nehemiah was heartbroken at the news of the Jewish remnant left in Jerusalem. The people were scattered and the wall surrounding the city had been broken down, its gates burned. For days he mourned, wept, and prayed. In the soil of a repentant, God-loving heart, the Lord gave Nehemiah the seed of a dream (see Neh. 2:12).

Nehemiah prayed for God's guidance and success as he confronted his first challenge of asking the king to send him to Jerusalem so that he could rebuild the wall—a particularly tricky request since the king himself had ordered the work on the wall to be stopped.

Nehemiah's goal began with prayer and was sustained through constant moment-by-moment prayer and guidance from God. God answered in abundance. The king not only allowed Nehemiah to go to Jerusalem; he also made him governor of Judea and provided him with letters that would allow him safe passage and the ability to get supplies for his project.

Once there Nehemiah took immediate action. He assessed the damage to the wall and began to talk to people about the mission God had laid on his heart. Support and enthusiasm came from leaders and common people alike. Even goldsmiths and merchants labored on the wall and laid bricks, but despite the support the going was not smooth. Opposition to his plan began immediately. He and the other laborers were laughed at, scorned, slandered, persecuted, threatened, and deceived. When the wall was halfway done, discouragement and exhaustion endangered the completion of the project. In the face of this and every other obstacle Nehemiah prayed, watched, and worked on toward his goal.

Incredibly, in only fifty-two days, the wall was rebuilt. This awesome accomplishment was only the beginning. The stage was now set for revival and repopulation of Jerusalem.

THE POWER OF GODLY GOALS

Nehemiah's goals were godly goals. Therefore, God was with him every step of the way. His goal originated out of prayer and communion with God, and his mission was accomplished with God's guidance and protection. Along the way Nehemiah and the other laborers did their part by working hard: "So we built the wall and the whole wall was joined together to half its height, for the people had a mind to work" (Neh. 4:6 NASB). As they were attacked on every level, Nehemiah prayed constantly and specifically, and God answered his prayers.

They were all trying to frighten us, thinking, "Their hands will get too weak for the work, and it will not be completed." But I prayed, "Now strengthen my hands." (Neh. 6:9)

It was a mammoth project; the odds against it were huge; it was more than mere men could accomplish. In other words, it was the perfect situation to glorify God.

Christians sometimes struggle with goal setting, fearing that the process undermines God's will for a person's life and indicates a desire to control the future. As believers we are to place our trust in God, not worry about the future, and allow the Holy Spirit to guide our steps. That's why loving God with our entire being is essential to setting godly goals. When our hearts are brimming with love for God, we can wholly trust the desires of our heart.

Delight yourself in the LORD *and he*
will give you the desires of your heart. (Ps. 37:4)

> When God is going to
> do a wonderful thing, he
> begins with a difficulty.
> When he is going to
> do a very wonderful
> thing, he begins with
> an impossibility!
> —CHARLES INWOOD

For some, the idea that God *wants* us to have our deep desires is truly a revolutionary concept. We may have been raised to believe that God is the big killjoy in the sky. However, if we doubt the appropriateness of our desires, that may signal a divided heart and the need to draw closer to the Lord. If you can answer an unreserved *yes* when you ask yourself if your desires glorify God, you can confidently follow your heart.

The Bible encourages us to plan. The Book of Proverbs is filled with wisdom on the subjects of planning and working diligently:

A sluggard does not plow in season;
so at harvest time he looks but finds nothing. (Prov. 20:4)
The plans of the diligent lead to profit
as surely as haste leads to poverty. (21:5)
Do not those who plot evil go astray?
But those who plan what is good find
love and faithfulness. (14:22)
Commit to the LORD *whatever you do,*
and your plans will succeed. (16:3)

Our plans and goals should be consistent with God's sovereign and moral will for our lives and born out of a desire to love and serve others. Psalm 127:1 reminds us that "unless the LORD builds the house, its builders labor in vain." The same holds true for our goals. Unless the Lord directs them and is glorified through them, our efforts will be in vain. As we set our goals, we should ask God to guide our thoughts and desires, and pray that he will give us wisdom and discernment as we live to honor him.

After praying for God's leading, we should ask ourselves what we value most in life. If what we value most contradicts our goals, this is a red flag that guarantees inner conflict and struggle in the decision-making process. Eventually, physical and emotional exhaustion will take their toll on us. Our goals, and the plan we make to reach them, should be con-

> *With the goodness of God to desire our highest welfare, the wisdom of God to plan it, what do we lack?*
> —A. W. TOZER

sistent with our values. In the following story Steve's desire to succeed at work failed to consider this and resulted in turmoil.

"But Daddy! Why can't you come to my soccer game tomorrow?"

Steve hugged Amber and brushed her hair away from her eyes. "I'm sorry, baby, but I have to go out of town for my job. That's what makes it possible for us to live in our house and pay our bills."

Amber fidgeted and looked at the floor.

"Do you understand, baby?" he asked. "You know I'd be there if I could."

Steve hated the way he felt. He loved going to his children's games and school activities, and for months he had missed one activity after another.

Recently he had set new goals at work. He wanted to add three new accounts each month, increase his annual income by 10 percent, and eventually be promoted to sales manager. For the first two months he progressed in his goals and was pleased with the results, but after a while Steve's motivation began to wane and so did his results. He noticed that for the first time in years he was not happy at work. His heavy travel schedule made leisurely talks with his wife a rarity. Being gone on the weekends made it difficult for him to attend church, and working late meant he had to miss his children's soccer games. He felt frustrated and discouraged.

When Steve thought about it, he realized that the most important things in his life were his marriage, his children, and his relationship with God. These values had always served as a sort of internal compass that helped him make decisions. When he set his new goals for work, he realized he would have to work later and travel more frequently, but the desire to progress in his work and make a good living was a strong motivation. Now as he considered the situation, the problem became clear. *No wonder I'm dissatisfied*, he thought. *I've set goals that contradict my values.* If he got the position of sales manager, his permanent job would be based on travel. The larger salary would be nice, but it wouldn't make up for the loss of time with his family.

Once he could articulate the problem, he changed his promotion goals to eventually become the operations manager, a position that would have less prestige and a smaller salary but would mean a more flexible schedule with his family. It would take some retraining and night classes, but the short-term sacrifice would mean long-term gain.

COUNT THE COST

Steve's intentions were good, but when he made his initial goals, he had failed to count the cost. Jesus knew that people are prone to making emotional and hasty decisions. When he was talking with the crowds, they surely must have been captivated and tempted to follow him. Rather than urge them toward an impulsive decision, Jesus told them to slow down and count the cost of being his disciples. To illustrate the danger of hasty action, he gave a very tangible illustration.

"Suppose one of you wants to build a tower. Will he not
first sit down and estimate the cost to see if he has enough
money to complete it? For if he lays the foundation and is not
able to finish it, everyone who sees it will ridicule him,
saying, 'This fellow began to build and was not able to finish.'"
(Luke 14:28–30)

Blueprints, supply lists, and time lines are essential for building a home. These same principles of planning apply to setting goals. Once we have prayed for God's leading and have identified our values, we can ask ourselves what we want to accomplish in our walk with God, our career, finances, health, family, marriage, education, and other areas. When our goals are defined, we can begin listing the logical steps needed to accomplish them. For instance, if your career goal is to become an elementary schoolteacher, your list of objectives may include selecting a college or university, completing the application process, working part-time at a child development center while you're in school, and graduating with a degree in elementary education.

Fulfilling our dreams can be a long and difficult process. It requires sacrifice, hard work, and persistence—three things that initially create discomfort but ultimately bring immense satisfaction. The bigger the dream, the bigger the potential reward.

Farmers know they can't expect a bountiful harvest unless they have generously seeded their crops. "Whoever sows sparingly will also reap sparingly, and whoever sows generously will also reap generously" (2 Cor. 9:6). In the context of Scripture this metaphor illustrates the rewards of generous giving. This principle is valid in other areas as well. If we sow the seeds of carefully and prayerfully planned goals, we increase our chances of reaping an abundant harvest of good works and fulfillment.

Small measures can also bring surprisingly big rewards. Committing our goals to writing increases the probability of obtaining them by up to 80 percent. When our goals are firmly planted in our minds, we begin to subconsciously make decisions that carry us toward the reality. And when we verbalize our goals to encouraging people we trust, we are creating a network of prayer and support. By the same token, there will be people who don't want us to succeed and therefore, should not be entrusted with our dreams.

FAILURE'S REWARD

Everyone stumbles from time to time, and sometimes we even fall flat on our faces. A temporary setback or even an outright failure doesn't have to halt the quest for our dream. God sees beyond our failures to our potential. Unfortunately, we are not so forgiving with ourselves. We can overreact and conclude: "My ministry is over—God will never forgive me"; "My kids will be damaged for life"; "I'll never accomplish anything." We need to acknowledge our failures and to grieve the loss associated with them, but we must allow God to use the experience as he works on growing us into godly men and women. We can accomplish this only by strengthening our faith and trusting in a merciful God.

The eleventh chapter of Hebrews is often referred to as the "faith chapter." Included in this chapter is a long list of ordinary men and women whom God used to accomplish extraordinary things by faith. These people were not perfect. In fact, Noah was guilty of alcohol abuse and immorality. Abraham lied and took matters into his own hands. Sarah doubted God and could be selfish and cruel. Jacob lied and was not above cheating. The list of failures goes on. God could have forgotten these people and cast them aside, but he didn't. Instead, he used them and accomplished great things through them, despite their shortcomings. In Hebrews 11:34, we read that sometimes their weaknesses were actually turned into strengths under God's merciful hand. Regardless of our failures and weaknesses, God wants to use us if we will surrender our will to him.

> *God is a specialist; he is well able to work our failures into his plans . . . often the doorway to success is entered through the hallway of failure.*
> —ERWIN W. LUTZER

Whatever plans we make, we must keep in mind that, ultimately, God is in control. To experience true success, we must rely on him to direct our thoughts, guide our steps, and give us the will to remain committed and persevere.

Our faith may waver when the future looks unclear or threatening. Corrie ten Boom faced unimaginable hardship and persecution at the hands of the Nazis during World Ward II. From one moment to the next, her life could have ended; yet this incredible woman lived through it, and her faith strengthened to the point that she could confidently say, "Never be afraid to trust an unknown future to a known God."

As you briefly travel in others' shoes through the following stories, we hope that you will be encouraged to trust your future to a knowing and loving God. Together may you reap a rich harvest from your own field of dreams.

Anne could hear the phone ringing in her dorm room as she fumbled for her keys. She pushed open the door and grabbed the receiver.

"Hello," she said breathlessly.

"You okay?"

"Hi, Evan," she took a deep breath. "I just ran for the phone."

She had met him recently at a Campus Crusade for Christ meeting and they had gone out together a few times. He was a nice guy and good company, but she knew right away that they would never be more than friends.

He invited her to a party Friday night at their group leader's house.

Even though she was a freshman in college, dating was still a little foreign to her. She had decided early on to set high standards and stick to them. In high school those high standards had given her a reputation that meant she wasn't asked out very often—she hadn't even gone to her senior prom.

When she was very young, she made her decision to remain a virgin until she married. Even back then she knew it wasn't the popular choice. But in middle school she attended a conference that featured Josh McDowell and his book *Why Wait?* He talked about what the Bible had to say about sex—how God had designed it to be a beautiful thing shared within marriage. It wasn't something dirty to be ashamed of, or something cheap to be carelessly given away. It was a sacred act of love between a husband and a wife.

She wanted that for herself and for her future husband. She was lucky to have several girlfriends who felt the same way, so throughout high school they had supported each other in their choice.

In their junior year they did a Bible study that focused on being godly young women. Their study leader encouraged them to be strong and to trust that God would reward their obedience.

"When you decide to be a woman after God's own heart, it brings the incredible bonus of being spared from many of life's sorrows and regrets. You won't have to deal with unwanted pregnancies, disease, or guilt. When it's time for you to marry, you can come to your husband free of the baggage that so many people drag into their relationships. You can present him with the unspoiled gift of yourself."

She then encouraged the girls to make a list of qualities they wanted in their future husband.

"Pray about it first and then be specific," she told them. "Someday you'll realize how faithful and delighted God is to give you the desires of your heart."

Anne knew without a doubt that the number one quality she wanted in her future husband was for him to be a Christian. It was also very important that they both were pure on their wedding day—so those two things topped the list. She wanted an affectionate man with a strong work ethic and a great sense of humor. Then she thought of her Bible study leader's challenge to be specific in her request. She had always loved the unusual combination of dark hair and blue eyes—she wrote it on her list. It was a tall order and she knew it—no one she had ever dated had even come close. She folded the paper and stuck it in the drawer. For years she never gave her list another thought.

On Friday night, Evan picked her up at her dorm. Anne took one look at him and said, "Oh, my gosh! How did you do that?"

He had played Frisbee in the park that afternoon. It had been such a warm day that he'd taken off his shirt and gotten horribly sunburned.

"It's my own fault," he said as he eased into the car. "I'm Swedish, if I don't wear sunscreen, I get toasted."

At the party, Evan shifted miserably as he sat next to her on the couch. Every time they started to talk, he grimaced and stood up to pull his shirt away from his back. "I'm sorry," he finally said, "but I'm in pain. I'd better head home."

Sarah, a friend from Anne's dorm, overheard their conversation. "I've got my car, Anne," she said. "Do you want to ride back with me later?"

Anne stayed. It was a small decision that would prove to have huge ramifications in her life.

About an hour later, several people arrived that Anne had never seen before at any of the meetings. One guy in particular caught her eye. Apparently, she caught his eye, too, because he gradually worked his way across the room and sat down beside her. He took off his baseball cap and ran his hand over his dark hair.

"Hi, I'm Michael. I've never seen you here before." He smiled at her. "I guess I'd better start coming to the meetings more regularly!"

She studied him. *What incredible blue eyes!*

After only a few weeks of dating, they both knew they'd found "the one," but they continued dating for a year and half before they were formally engaged.

One day, Anne found the list she had made in her high school Bible study. Just as the study leader said, God had generously answered her prayer. First and foremost, he had given her a man who was more than a Christian in name only. Michael was thoroughly committed to living his life for the Savior who had died for him.

Even though Anne and Michael were equally committed to being married before they made love for the first time, their fourteen-month engagement and deepening love put them to the test. There were times when they were dangerously tempted. In those instances, their shared convictions were the only way they were able to resist. As Michael said, "We'll have the rest of our lives together; let's not blow it now."

Through their premarital classes, they were developing the habit of praying together for their future and any problems they were currently facing. They made it a point to continually pray for strength to be obedient to God's Word in their personal relationship.

The church was lit with candles and hundreds of tiny white lights. The familiar sanctuary seemed transformed into something from another world. Anne's dress fell in luxurious waves of taffeta. From start to finish, their wedding ceremony was the expression of their love for God and for each other.

The only baggage they carried into their marriage was the matching luggage they took on their honeymoon. And what an incredible honeymoon it was. There were no silent jealousies and no hidden comparisons—only a strong love that cared enough to wait for the right person at the right time.

DETOURS TO A DREAM

Steve was in junior-high school when he first began to dream of becoming a lawyer. It was a big dream considering his humble roots. He was the oldest of five children. His father was a laborer in a lumber mill, and his mother was a secretary. But it was, in part, because of his modest circumstances that being a lawyer called to him. He was fascinated with the legal system and the way a lawyer could use his knowledge to help people who weren't able to help themselves.

His parents worried about the cost of college and law school, but Steve's grades were strong, and he felt certain he could get scholarships and grants. If he set his mind to it, what could possibly stop him?

But when he was sixteen, his father died in a logging accident. He and three other laborers were trying to unjam a log in the river when he was crushed. In that instant, the future was irreversibly changed for Steve and his family. The small life insurance policy barely covered the cost of the funeral.

As the oldest, Steve took a job as a stock clerk in a grocery store to help support the family. He was a good worker and the manager gave him all the hours he could handle. With Steve's help, the family was managing, but his grades suffered.

Although he graduated without a problem, his average grades kept him from being considered for a scholarship. He was disappointed, but he knew that even with financial help for college he couldn't leave now and ignore the needs of his family.

Two years, he told himself. *In two years, I'll be able to start college.*

Two years turned into five.

At twenty-three, his life wasn't what he thought it would be at this time, but there were some definite bright spots. Although he was still helping his mother, he had moved into a place of his own. He was enjoying his independence, and he was dating a very special girl he'd met at church. When his mother received several raises and promotions, Steve felt that he and Sylvia could get married.

After the wedding, they worked out a plan.

"When fall semester starts, I'll work part time and go to school full time. If all goes well, I'll go straight through, and by the time I'm thirty, I'll have my law degree," he said.

It seemed like a solid plan, but in his second year of college, there was an unexpected detour—Sylvia was pregnant. They were thrilled, but it was a difficult pregnancy and Sylvia had to quit working in her fifth month.

After their daughter was born, Steve had to return to working full time, but he managed to take a couple of classes. It was tough working all day and studying through the evenings. The only social life they managed to maintain was church on Sundays.

When their daughter was six months old, Sylvia started working thirty hours a week. It was a sacrifice, and Steve hated that she had to be away from the baby so long.

"Maybe it's not worth it," he said.

But Sylvia wouldn't let him consider giving up. "Just keep going," she said, "you'll get there eventually."

Three years later, at thirty years of age, Steve received his undergraduate degree.

They talked about waiting for a while before going to law school, but they decided not to put it off. He applied and was accepted.

Steve worked furiously for two years. It was still tough, but he was beginning to see a glimmer of light at the end of the tunnel. In his third year of law school, however, disaster struck. A pickup truck ran a stop sign and hit him broadside, pushing him into an oncoming lane of traffic where he was hit two more times.

With a severe concussion, two broken legs, facial lacerations, and a bruised liver, Steve was in the hospital for two weeks and rehab for six weeks. Once again school was on hold. He would be out for two semesters while he recovered.

Alone with Sylvia, his anger and confusion pushed him to despair. "I don't understand why God allowed this to happen to me. Ever since I was a kid and decided I wanted to be a lawyer, it's been one obstacle after another. Maybe it's time to read the handwriting on the wall and give up my dream."

Sylvia pressed her hand on his shoulder. "You'll regret it forever if you quit now. You're so close—one more year! You can do it."

The last year of law school is generally thought to be the easiest. For Steve it was absolutely the toughest. As a result of his accident, he had chronic back pain and headaches that prevented him from reading for more than thirty minutes at a stretch. It was a grueling, painful time, but finally, at the age of thirty-six, Steve graduated from law school!

He found a great job in a medium-sized firm, and with the settlement money from his accident, he was able to pay off all his undergraduate and law school student loans. At his lowest point following the accident, when he felt so abandoned, God was already working his plan to bring this blessing out of adversity.

Steve knows that pursuing a dream is sometimes a rough road that comes at a high cost. But he also knows that staying on course in spite of the potholes and detours brings an even sweeter satisfaction when you finally reach your dream.

ACCORDING TO HIS PLAN

Becky placed her journal, a small notebook, and a tape recorder in the suitcase on top of her clothes. She considered the portable typewriter. *Yes, might as well bring that along as well.* In the bathroom, she gathered all her prescription medications into a zippered plastic bag and placed them in the suitcase.

Katie bounded in from the hallway and jumped up on the bed.

"Mom, why do you have to go?" She lifted out the bag of medicines and held it up to the light studying it absently as though it were a kaleidoscope.

Becky snatched the bag out of her hand and Katie drew back, startled. Aware of her overreaction, Becky gently touched her daughter's cheek and replaced the bag under a folded sweatshirt.

"Honey," she said, "you know that every now and then I need to go to the cabin for a little time alone."

"But I don't want you to go. The fifth-graders are going on a field trip to the zoo tomorrow. I wish you could come and help like Sarah's mom."

Becky glanced at Katie, who was suddenly intent on examining her fingernails. They both knew that even if there had not been a trip planned to the cabin she still would not be one of the "helper moms" going to the zoo. A familiar heaviness settled around her heart. She lifted Katie's chin with her hand and looked at her softly. "I'm sorry, honey."

Katie forced a smile that didn't reach her brown eyes. "It's okay, Mom. Can I go next door to play for a while?"

Alone again, Becky angrily wrestled the suitcase closed. In spite of Katie's words, it was not okay! Nothing was okay! The years of fighting this relentless cancer had left her deeply weary and in constant pain. More and more her days were spent in bed. What good was she to her three children—to her husband—to God?

She had always dreamed of having a family to take care of and perhaps studying psychology so that she might have the opportunity to help others. But she was the one who needed care. And how could she help anyone when she was confined to her bed? She'd never thought her dreams were out of line or asking too much, but apparently God thought differently.

It was God's apparent indifference to her prayers that somehow validated Becky's decision to end her life. It had not been a hasty decision. She had thought about it and prayed about it for months. During this time, God had been silent. However, Becky didn't feel that his silence meant he hadn't heard her. On the contrary, she knew without a doubt that he was thoroughly acquainted with the exhaustion and pain that held her in despair and frustration. His silence just felt like sad acceptance. God knew her heart and her circumstances. He would understand her actions.

During the preceding months, she had arrived at a plan that she felt would be easiest on everyone. Because of her ongoing pain, she had ample prescription medication to accomplish a lethal overdose. After long consideration she decided to carry it out at the cabin. This would ensure that her children would not find her, and it would not leave their home tainted with images of her death.

The three-hour drive to the cabin on Lake Michigan soothed her. After months of mental struggle, she felt the peaceful resolve of a decision made and set in motion. She listened to music and thought about the letters she planned to write to her family and friends. She understood that people often feel guilty when someone they know and love commits suicide, but she would write to them, explain her decision, and tell them how much she loved them. Yes, it would still be hard on them, but eventually everyone would be better off.

The cabin's rustic wooden porch greeted her like an old friend. She stood in the doorway and looked around. Nothing had changed, she noted with satisfaction. The dusty blue davenport and worn coffee table and chairs still bore the comfortable look of years of the family's holiday use. There wasn't a nook or cranny that didn't hold a memory. How many times had she called the kids to the kitchen window to see a deer nibble on the grass or to watch a raccoon scramble up a tree? She felt tears sting her eyes. She pushed the thoughts from her mind and resumed an attitude of purpose.

Settling on the davenport, she arranged her writing materials and tape recorder. The letters must be finished tonight in one concentrated session of effort and focus. She had to pace her energy and emotions so that she would have the strength she needed. Tomorrow she would allow herself a drive to the family's favorite stretch of beach, and then she would return to the cabin and carry out what she had come to do.

The next morning, Becky awoke on the davenport still fully dressed. She rubbed her neck and surveyed the stack of envelopes on the coffee table. She had spent every ounce of energy writing them. Whatever sense of accomplishment she might have felt was offset by the somber task that still lay ahead. This would be a day like no other—the day her life would end.

She drove to the familiar beach on the shores of the lake. The bright morning sun contrasted the chill of early spring, and the secluded beach was a vision of desolate beauty. Becky rolled up the cuffs of her pants and took off her shoes and socks. The water was cold, but she didn't mind. She wanted to feel it once more.

As she strolled, she talked to God about her life, her love for him, and the circumstances that had brought her to this decision. She was accustomed to his silent presence; she had talked with him like this countless times.

A heavy fog suddenly rose up around her. It shrouded the clear day and muffled the air. No matter how she strained to see, the view was blocked like a hand before her face. The oppressive thickness aroused her claustrophobia bringing with it a mild sense of panic. Logic told her she could move if she chose to, but she stood still as though captured in an invisible web. Her perspective of the world had been reduced to the small patch of shore straight down into the water. She saw the rolled cuffs of her pants and watched the waves pull the sand from beneath her feet only to bring it and the tiny scurrying stones back up to the shore again.

At that moment, the inaudible, but unmistakably clear voice of God spoke to her, saying, "Do you see the waves rolling back and forth in the water and lapping onto the land? Do you see that the sand responds to the pull of the waves? The tiny stones and bits of glass are tempered and smoothed by constant movement. I have created these things, but they are mute. I order them to do as they are doing and they obey without question. You are my only creation that can voice opinions, question my will, and rebel against me. I'm asking you not to do that. Don't turn away from me. As long as you continue to face me, I will take all you have to give, whether anger, sorrow, pain, disappointment, or joy. I won't ever abandon you."

A hole was suddenly cut in the fog, and the sun shone through, washing Becky in a shower of light. Then, as quickly as it had come, the fog receded and vanished.

Four years have passed since that morning on the beach. Becky returned to her home, her family, and her battle with cancer. From her bed, she spends her time talking with her children and family, and she treasures every conversation. Over the years she has taken several psychology courses. She reads and studies, when she's able.

Much of her time is spent on the phone. Someone will call and ask Becky if she will talk to a friend who is struggling with cancer. She always does. Her counsel is real and honest, and encourages them in a way that no one else could. Sometimes she recognizes a familiar despondency in their voice. That's when she tells about her plan to end her life and God's saving presence and promises on the shore of Lake Michigan.

Becky's dreams haven't come true in the way she had planned, but they have come true according to God's plan for her life. She relies heavily on God's promise that he is in everything that happens, and he will never abandon her. Like the waves on the shore, Becky knows that God is the One to direct her coming in and going out.

- Our dreams can take us where we want to go if we will courageously combine them with action and trust the outcome to God.
- The fulfillment of a dream begins with knowing what it will look like once we've obtained it.
- Setting goals is important but praying, as we set them, is essential.
- When we are walking with God and are obedient to his Word, we can trust the desires of our heart.
- The most beneficial and realistic goals are those that are consistent with what we value most in life.
- Worthwhile goals can only be achieved by our willingness to work hard, delay gratification, and persevere in the face of adversity.
- Goals and dreams should be shared only with those people who will support us and cheer us on to victory.
- As we commit our plans and dreams to the Lord, he will guide our steps and direct our actions.
- Goals are like a road map: the more detailed they are, the more likely we are to arrive at our desired destination.
- Sometimes God allows the path of our dreams to lead to a dead end so that we might turn around and let him direct us toward a new purpose of greater value to his kingdom.

4

Marriage: For Better, For Worse, For Good

By wisdom a house is built, and through understanding
it is established; through knowledge its rooms
are filled with rare and beautiful treasures.
PROVERBS 24:3–4

Julie was a typical bride-to-be. She planned her wedding with studied attention. From her elegantly simple wedding gown to the hand-calligraphed place cards for the tables, she made each decision with care. Julie and Dennis spent hours together talking about their honeymoon and shopping for an apartment. Sometimes they disagreed, but against the backdrop of their exciting plans and glowing future, they always managed to compromise and settle the matter quickly.

Julie knew that Dennis didn't share her Christian beliefs; however, he was interested in spiritual matters and agreed that their children should be raised in a home where church was a priority.

And Dennis would be a good provider. He graduated in the top 10 percent of his class in law school, and his efforts were rewarded when he was offered a promising position in a large, prestigious firm.

When Julie pictured their marriage, she envisioned romantic dinners, leisurely walks, and stimulating conversations. If she was upset, he would comfort her and hold her through the night. When she awoke in the morning, he would tell her she was beautiful. She felt certain that Dennis would make all her dreams come true.

Ten years later Julie's dreams have been overshadowed by the nightmare of their failed marriage and tumultuous divorce. The closeness she had expected seemed as short-lived as the honeymoon. Like so many of their plans, attending church fell to the wayside as the constant demands and stresses of children, home, and Dennis's billable hours took precedence.

Julie is now in her thirties and struggling to raise two young children on her own while holding down a job. She looks back on her marriage and wonders, "What went wrong? Why did my marriage fail?"

THE COLD, HARD FACTS

Unfortunately, Julie's story is not unique. Although statistics are sometimes misleading, it's clear that American couples are divorcing at an alarming rate. According to the National Center for Health Statistics, in 1997 alone more than one million married couples were granted a divorce. This number exceeded the previous record-breaking year for divorces that took place in 1985.

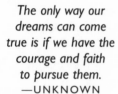

The only way our dreams can come true is if we have the courage and faith to pursue them.
—UNKNOWN

In light of these statistics, it's not surprising that more and more people are choosing the single life over marriage. Ironically, even many single people have experienced a divorce—through the failed marriage of their parents. They know all too well that sometimes the best intentions cannot withstand the challenges that come with marriage. Still there are countless men and woman who admit they would love to marry and have a union that would last for a lifetime, but fear and doubt keep them from making the choice.

The specter of divorce haunts the single and married alike. Many married couples are so aware of the odds against them that they feel insecure even though their marriage seems stable. They look around and see their friends divorcing—didn't their marriages appear solid too? It seems as though divorce strikes like lightening—indiscriminately and with deadly results.

Others are actively struggling with challenges in their marriage. The hopes and dreams they brought into the marriage have now been replaced with confusion and disappointment. As their problems persist, their vows seem less like sacred promises and more like a life sentence they must serve.

These situations beg the questions: Is there true hope for fulfilling marriages in our day and age? Is it possible for couples to avoid or reduce the challenges and problems that come their way by learning and implementing time-tested wisdom and biblical truths regarding marriage? The answer to both questions is yes!

GETTING THE BIG PICTURE

One of God's greatest gifts to men and women is marriage. He wants us to delight in the pleasure and intimacy that a loving marriage brings. In order to experience the joys of a godly marriage, it helps to understand what God had in mind when he created man, woman, and marriage. When we see the "big picture," we are less prone to look only for the fulfillment of our own needs and desires and, instead, learn how to get in line with the Master's design for marriage.

A MIRROR IMAGE

God had a plan for men and women from the time of creation. The first chapter of Genesis tells us a great deal about the purpose of our lives. After creating the earth and the animals, God said:

> *"Let us make man in our image, in our likeness, and let them*
> *rule over the fish of the sea and the birds of the air, over the*
> *livestock, over all the earth, and over all the creatures that move*
> *along the ground." So God created man in his own image, in the*
> *image of God he created him; male and female he created them.*
> (Gen. 1:26–27)

God's first purpose for creating man was to mirror his image on earth. Rather than mirroring a physical likeness, our hearts are to reflect God. When our hearts are right with him, our behaviors will magnify, exalt, and glorify God. We are to rule over the earth with the hand of a trusted caretaker, using wisdom and discernment. But God didn't stop there.

ALONE NO MORE

When Adam was carrying out his task of naming the animals, he must have noticed that each animal had a male and female counterpart. Yet he lacked a mate of his own. In Genesis 2, the Lord made his first negative statement regarding his creation.

The LORD God said, "It is not good for the man to be alone.
I will make a helper suitable for him." (Gen. 2:18)

Adam's life was already full. His needs were met, he lived in beauty, and he had rewarding work and awesome communion with God. Yet Adam felt alone. We can conclude that man has a fundamental need for companionship. In spite of all he had already given him, God wanted Adam to live in *complete* fulfillment.

When God met Adam's need by creating Eve, Adam was at no loss for words to express his delight with his new mate. "This is now bone of my bones and flesh of my flesh" (Gen. 2:23). The meaning of "this is now" can best be expressed as "At last!" The unnamed yearning was finally met. Adam recognized his counterpart immediately; she was much like himself, only wonderfully different.

> *The goal in marriage is not to think alike but to think together.*
> —UNKNOWN

This wonderful difference is still the source of much delight and much trouble between the sexes. Each man and woman brings to their marriage a unique package of personal experiences, talents, abilities, and distinct personality traits that, when combined, have the potential of forming an exciting and fulfilling bond. Ironically these same factors also have the potential of bringing trials, unmet expectations, and the need for selfless acceptance and love.

DIVINE INTERDEPENDENCE

What did God have in mind when he brought man and woman together in marriage? Were they simply to keep one another company while selfishly pursuing their own goals, or were they to selflessly abandon their dreams in deference to the needs of their mate? Neither of these extremes were God's plan.

When writing to the first-century church in Corinth, Paul discussed the need for healthy *interdependence* within marriage. "In the Lord, however, woman is not independent of man, nor is man independent of woman" (1 Cor. 11:11). This underscores the fact that the individuals in the marriage possess both a component of need and a component of strength that is balanced under the hand of the Lord. There is, therefore, a great interchange of love, trust, and support that flow between husband and wife.

Some people, however, choose to live their lives independent of their mates. In doing so, they deprive themselves and their spouses of the intimacy God intended. On the other hand, overdependence on each other can stifle personal growth and limit what the individuals have to offer within marriage. Both independence and overdependence deny the rich fulfillment God intended. As the Scripture indicates, where there is balance and mutuality, there will also be peace and fulfillment.

> *We are not placed on this earth to see through each other, but to see each other through.*
> —WILLIAM KINNAIRD

AN UNCOMMON LOVE

In his letter to the Ephesians, Paul expands on God's plan for husbands and wives. Marriage is compared to Christ's relationship to the church, which he refers to as his bride.

Husbands, love your wives, just as Christ loved the church and gave himself up for her to make her holy, cleansing her by the washing with water through the word, and to present her to himself as a radiant church, without stain or wrinkle or any other blemish, but holy and blameless. In this same way, husbands ought to love their wives as their own bodies. He who loves his wife loves himself. After all, no one ever hated his own body, but he feeds and cares for it, just as Christ does the church—for we are members of his body. "For this reason a man will leave his father and mother and be united to his wife, and the two will become one flesh." This is a profound mystery—but I am talking about Christ and the church. However, each one of you also must love his wife as he loves himself, and the wife must respect her husband. (Eph. 5:25–33)

The Scriptures present a balance of truth. God gives instruction both to the husband and wife for achieving a godly marriage. In a union between believers, it is the combination of a loving, submissive wife (Eph. 5:22) coupled with a husband who cares for her with a sacrificial love that are the primary keys for lasting marriage. In living out these characteristics in our marriage, we gain a deep union with our mate and an understanding of the profound love Christ has for the church.

In our society, *submission* is not a politically correct word. The idea of caring for one another with an attitude of deference is almost unheard of. In the Scriptures, however, submission never implies inferiority. Jesus is submissive to God the Father (Luke 22:42) but certainly not inferior to him. Similarly, the church is willingly submissive to Christ, the Head, in part because he demonstrated his great love for us by sacrificing himself on the cross so that we might live.

> *Part of what it means to be God's children is to accept what he knows, and that he will bring what is best into our lives—not what we want every time, but what is ultimately best for us.*
> —CHARLES PAUL CONN

Unfortunately, some husbands have used the "submission Scriptures" as weapons of control. Like a carelessly handled gun, this can bring devastating results. Submission becomes infinitely more understandable when a husband loves his wife unconditionally and with an attitude of self-sacrifice. A wife married to such a husband would have no fear of submitting to him because she would know his love for her was deep, sacrificial, and selfless.

Sadly, at the core of most marital problems is not selflessness but rather selfishness and pride—the two basic traits that make up our fallen human nature. Both men and women tend to focus on what they can get from their relationship rather than on what they can give. Therefore, they often measure the success of the marriage by the fulfillment of their own needs.

God knew that there would be conflict and problems between two individuals, so he gave us the tools to work out our differences in a healthy framework. Originally, God designed the home to be like a greenhouse—a warm, nurturing place where husband, wife, and children would thrive. In this atmosphere, problems can be dealt with in mutual love and respect. Children grow up seeing that hard times come and go, but the Christ-centered marriage survives. God's Word is revered and implemented in an everyday way. Conveying this message to our children is one of our most important purposes of marriage. In Psalm 78, the psalmist encouraged parents to honor God's command to teach their children about his faithfulness so that future generations might also put their confidence in God. Through the lines of godly descendants, Satan's efforts are thwarted.

Thinking back to the disheartened Julie, it becomes clear that her marriage was on perilous ground from the beginning. Compromise is often a good and wise thing to do, but there is no room for compromise when we are choosing a mate for life. Standing firm in a decision to marry another believer is a vital link to a successful, godly marriage.

> *Christ is not valued at all unless he is valued above all else.*
> —ST. AUGUSTINE

As you read the stories that follow, you will have the benefit of both the wise and the not-so-wise decisions of others. In either case, you have the great privilege of learning lessons that may apply in your own life and marriage.

THE PROMISE

"Mrs. Emerson?" asked a male voice over the phone.

"Yes," Ellen answered.

"Do you know where your husband is?"

"Who is this?"

"You don't know me," he said flatly. "Do you know where your husband is?"

"Of course I do; he's at work."

"No. He's not," said the voice.

"How do you know?" asked Ellen.

There was a pause.

"Because he's with my wife."

Ellen hung up the phone and grabbed the stair banister for support. This must be some kind of sick joke. But when Sean came home from work and she confronted him, the joke became a nightmare.

They had been married for twenty-five years. They'd raised two children together; they had buried three of their parents; they had laughed; they had loved; they had promised—he had promised!

Ellen cried. "How could you do this to me?"

"I tried to tell you I was unhappy," Sean said.

"When? And even if you did, does that give you the right to cheat on me? Sean, you know this is wrong—it's wrong in God's eyes. You have to stop this!"

Sean eventually promised to end the affair and work on their marriage. At first, his efforts seemed forced and mechanical, and she was so hurt she could scarcely stand to look at him. Nothing about their life seemed genuine or sacred anymore. Even insignificant activities like Sean going to the grocery story without her became areas where trust had to be established from scratch. It was a long, painful process. Little by little, healing began and Ellen started to trust Sean again.

Almost a year later, Ellen answered the phone on a Saturday morning. A sickeningly familiar voice said, "Mrs. Emerson, they're together again."

With Sean that night she yelled, "You promised you would end it! You're going to have to choose. Choose right now; her or me."

Sean couldn't look at her when he quietly answered, "I choose her."

He felt he should leave immediately, but Ellen insisted he stay the night.

"We have twenty-five years invested in one another. Are you going to just throw that away? Think about this! Pray about this!"

As she lay in bed, tears streamed down her face as she prayed, "Lord, I've been your faithful daughter. How could you allow this to happen to me?"

Sean left the next morning, but to Ellen's surprise he came back that night. He set his suitcase in the foyer and said simply, "She's decided to stay with her husband."

The next few days were surreal. Sean was home, but that fact was devoid of victory or hope. Nothing could dispel Ellen's hurt and the betrayal she felt. After confiding in their pastor, he referred them to a Christian counselor. Ellen knew it was good for them to be reminded of God's plan for husbands and wives, but after several visits, both she and Sean felt they had reached an impasse.

Before all this had come out into the open, Sean had planned to go to a Promise Keepers meeting with some of the men from their church over the weekend. All Ellen knew about Promise Keepers was that it was a Christ-centered ministry that encouraged men to lead lives of integrity. Both the timing and the irony were not lost on Ellen, but she encouraged him to go; she needed some time alone to try to sort out her feelings.

She pulled the drape away from the window and watched as he drove out of sight.

"Lord," she prayed, "our marriage is in ashes, yet you know I still love this man. I relinquish him and our marriage to you. We're in your hands."

Sean returned home with a new resolve and commitment to make their marriage work. He said that his experience at Promise Keepers had hit him between the eyes. He tried to convince Ellen that his commitment to her and their marriage was sincere. For once, he made no excuses. He apologized to her and admitted that he had broken his vows and been in blatant disobedience to God.

"I know it will take time for you to trust me again, honey," said Sean, "but I'm going to be here for you—I promise."

Promise! thought Ellen. It had once been a word that brought comfort; now it was a reminder of broken trust and her own broken heart.

The days and weeks passed. Sean suggested that they enroll in a couples' Bible study on marriage. "We've done marriage our way," said Sean. "Now let's find out what God really had in mind."

Ellen was reluctant, but as she looks back on it, she sees that this was the beginning of growth and healing for them both. Once she was able to see past her own hurts, she began to realize that she had become complacent in their marriage and toward Sean. She looked at him with fresh eyes and could see that he had felt unappreciated and unloved. Although Sean had broken the vows of their marriage, she could also see that she had neglected her own promises and responsibilities.

It was a bright, warm Sunday. A small gathering of friends and family congregated at the altar. Sean and Ellen held hands, looked into each other's eyes, and renewed their vows. The words seemed to penetrate Ellen's heart as she and her husband promised to always love and honor one another.

Ellen had prayed and asked God to somehow repair their broken marriage—and take all the shattered pieces and put them together in some semblance of what it once had been. But God didn't do that.

The Book of Isaiah says that the Lord will "comfort all who mourn, and provide for those who grieve in Zion—to bestow on them a crown of beauty instead of ashes, the oil of gladness instead of mourning, and garment of praise instead of a spirit of despair" (Isa. 61:3). God took the useless ashes of a dead marriage and made something beautiful and new. Only the Lord could make such a promise; only the Lord could keep it so perfectly.

LIGHT AND DARKNESS

When Shelby first started dating Stan, she had no intention of marrying him. She was an accountant, and they met when she was assigned to conduct the annual audit at the manufacturing plant where he worked. He was funny and attractive; she didn't see any reason why they shouldn't have lunch together occasionally. When the time came for her to settle down, she knew she wanted to marry a Christian, but she wasn't looking for a husband right now.

Stan wasn't at all interested in spiritual things, but he knew she was a Christian, and it didn't seem to bother him in the least. She privately hoped that he would become curious and interested in God through his friendship with her. He had decent morals and was such a nice person. Maybe through her, he would come to see his need for Christ.

Shelby was irritated when her family and friends at church were upset to learn she was dating someone who wasn't a Christian. By this time she and Stan really were dating. The lunches had gradually become dinners, and soon they were seeing a great deal of each other. She finally had to admit that she was falling in love with him.

When she told her brother about her feelings for Stan, Brian reacted with rigid disapproval.

"You have to step away from that relationship right now, Shelby. Believers are not to be yoked together with unbelievers; it's the ultimate mismatch! The Bible says, 'What does a believer have in common with an unbeliever? . . . What fellowship can light have with darkness?'"

She had heard the same thing from her friends at church. But how could she just turn away from the man she loved? She told herself that love had to be good. Her solution was to spend more time with Stan and less time at church and with her disapproving family.

When Stan asked her to marry him, she talked with him again about the difference in their beliefs. But he didn't see it as a problem.

"I would never stand in your way when you want to go church or spend time reading your Bible. That's fine with me. I don't want to change you," he said, "I love you the way you are."

Hadn't she waited all her life to hear those wonderful words? Deep in her heart she felt that after living with the influence of a Christian wife for a while, Stan would be drawn to the faith and choose to accept Christ. She had heard similar stories in church and she loved Stan so much! She prayed that somehow love would see them through, and she agreed to marry him.

For the first few years, things went relatively well. Shelby was sad when she got up on Sunday mornings and went to church alone. In fact, it was much harder than she had anticipated. She would look at the couples sitting side-by-side in church. How she envied marriages where husbands and wives could openly discuss the Lord and pray together about their problems. Still she had faith that Stan would eventually come around.

When they had been married four years, Shelby had a miscarriage. It was tough on both of them—they had been so excited at the prospect of being parents. Stan, however, looked at it as a personal attack from God.

"If God is so loving, how could he allow something like this to happen?"

She tried to help him understand. "God didn't do this to us. It's just one of those sad facts of life."

Although she tried to reassure him, it was a turning point for Stan and for their marriage. He began to resent every moment she was away with Bible study or church activities. He was jealous when she spent time with Christian friends or even her own family. She suspected that his unspoken but greatest jealousy was knowing that her first love would always be God.

When she reminded him of his promise not to interfere with her faith, he said, "That was then; this is now. Things are different."

For the first time, Shelby realized her hope of seeing Stan become a Christian might never come to pass. His behavior was steadily degenerating. He began going to bars and wanting her to go with him. If she refused, he was furious, yet when she went, she felt in conflict with her own values and beliefs. They argued constantly.

Now the mere sight of her Bible or a Christian book was all it took to start an argument between them. When her friends from church called, she had to tell them she would call them back when Stan wasn't there. Finally, in a desperate attempt to please her husband, she stopped going to church altogether.

Even with these measures, she and Stan spent more and more time apart. Then, after nine years of marriage, Stan told Shelby he no longer loved her and filed for divorce.

As heartbroken as she was, Shelby realized that her own stubbornness and pride had prompted her to ignore the Bible and the advice of trusted friends and family and marry an unbeliever in the first place. Not only had she hurt herself, she had hurt Stan too. Rather than being the catalyst that brought him to Christ, she may have actually been a factor that widened the gap between him and God. She loved Stan and wanted their marriage to succeed. Although she knows that won't happen, she still prays that Stan will eventually come to know the Lord.

Today she would never consider dating anyone who was not a Christian. She understands that when God told his children not to be yoked together with unbelievers he wasn't being narrow and confining. He was being kind and protective.

Perhaps the day will come that she marries again; time will tell. For now, she's enjoying the freedom of an unrestricted walk with the Lord. It's been an unexpected joy, like stepping out of the darkness and into the glorious light.

Return in Kind

Amanda smiled at Gram as she watched the eighty-three-year-old hands deftly roll out a crust for a cherry pie. She came up beside her grandmother and squeezed her shoulders. "Having you here is the best Christmas present I could ever have!" said Amanda.

Gram giggled and placed a dot of flour on the tip of Amanda's nose. "Well, you have your sweet husband to thank for that. He arranged everything—made my reservation, bought the ticket—even called Mrs. Sweeney next door and asked her to feed Daisy while I was gone."

Amanda sighed and shook her head. "It's the first time he's ever done anything like this in the three years we've been married." Then she added flatly, "I didn't know he had it in him. He's usually clueless about what I need."

Gram looked up from her piecrust, her smile faltered momentarily. "By the way, where is Sam?" she asked lightly.

"Probably working on something out in the garage," said Amanda as she rinsed dishes in the sink. "That's where he spends most of his time these days."

Gram looked up, her brow knit in concern.

Amanda went on. "He piddles around and makes little things with his woodworking tools."

Her grandmother turned back to her task. "You're so lucky to have a handy husband!" She rolled the crust onto the wooden rolling pin and placed it over the pie plate as she talked. "Why, my sweet Walter, bless his soul, he couldn't nail two boards together! Used to just drive me crazy! And of course my sister Emma's husband was a whiz at that kind of thing—made a hand-carved cradle for John Jr., and one Christmas he made Emma the most beautiful cedar chest I ever laid my eyes on. I was just green with envy!" She laughed a merry laugh. "Of course, you know I always was jealous of whatever Emma had, and poor Walter did the suffering for it."

"Oh, Gram," said Amanda, "I never noticed Gramp suffering any because of you."

"He did when we were first married, child! I promise you that!"

Amanda dried her hands and sat down at the table. "But he always called you his queen! I thought you two had the perfect marriage."

"Not at first," said Gram, resolutely shaking her head. "No, sir! I'll tell you something that most of the family doesn't know, but you have to promise not to tell."

"I promise," said Amanda.

"Well, we'd been married just a couple of years, when your Grandpa packed his bags one day and set them out on the porch. Then he came into the kitchen and took me by the shoulders and looked deep into my eyes. He said, 'Hannah, I love you, but I'm gonna have to quit you. I just can't take your harping and nagging a minute more! I'm not gonna live my life in a fuss.'"

"I can't believe it!" said Amanda. "I never heard you criticize him or say anything that could remotely be called nagging."

"Well, I had to learn different. I prayed to the good Lord to help me stop. You know the Harding women all come with sharp tongues—your own mama was like that—I'm sure I don't have to tell you! And your Aunt Elizabeth—mercy! I think Ed died young because there was no other way to get a moment's peace!"

"Gram! I can't believe you're saying this! I've never heard you say a word against anyone in the family before."

"I'm not gossiping, child. I'm telling you something that I believe you need to know." Gram wiped her hands on her apron and sat down at the table. "Now, I'm gonna ask you something, and if I'm out of line, you just tell me to hush, and I will. Okay?"

Amanda nodded.

"You and Sam are having problems, aren't you?"

Amanda's face contorted and tears burned her eyes. "Yes, Gram—we're having bad problems. How did you know?"

"Well, for one thing, when Sam was arranging to bring me here for your Christmas surprise, he said it was the only thing he could think of that might make you happy. That was a big hint, right there. And then there's that old problem of the Harding women and their sharp tongues. I'd seen signs of it in you that last time I visited."

"Really? When? What do you mean?" asked Amanda.

"Your poor Sam couldn't do anything right. One evening he laid a beautiful fire in the fireplace, but all you did was scold him for tracking in dirt. Then he was telling us about something funny that happened at work, and you turned to me and said, 'Sam shouldn't try to tell jokes—he has no sense of humor.' You said that right in front of him like he wasn't even there! Why, I looked over at your husband, and it liked to broke my heart—he was so hurt and embarrassed. Let me ask you, honey, would you talk that way to a friend? Would you ever be so blunt and unkind to a stranger? He's your husband; he deserves your respect in private and especially in public!"

Amanda started to cry. "Oh, Gram! What am I going to do? I think Sam's about to ask me for a divorce."

"When your Grandpa told me he was gonna quit me, it was like a light came on in my heart. I swallowed every bit of my pride, and I told him I loved him and that with the help of the Lord I was gonna change my ways. I won't kid you, it wasn't easy at first, and it won't be for you, either. Every time you're tempted to criticize or correct Sam, ask God to help you hold your tongue. And then ask the Lord to show you something in your husband to be thankful for—something to appreciate in him—and then tell him about it. Thank him for laying a beautiful fire even if he left a trail of twigs to the fireplace. Be kind to him, Amanda, and I guarantee he'll return in kind to you!"

Starting from that moment, Amanda began to follow Gram's advice. At first, it was all she could do to keep her mouth shut when a sarcastic or critical comment threatened to fly. But gradually she began to speak words of kindness and affirmation to a baffled but very pleased Sam.

What a shame that Gram didn't get to meet her darling great-granddaughter and namesake, Hannah. But her wisdom would reach through the generations—Amanda would see to that. The day might even come when Amanda needed to share those wise words with her own little girl—because you know about those Harding women—they all come with sharp tongues!

⌒ ⌒

LOOKING BACK ON LESSONS LEARNED

- If we choose a mate based upon God's principles and criteria, we will avoid many sorrows and regrets.
- When we are lonely, it's especially difficult to wait for God's best for us in a spouse; however, the rewards and pleasures will far surpass the pain of waiting and will last a lifetime.
- Every marriage has challenges. The keys to overcoming them include focusing on the Lord, staying unified in our goals and dreams, and remaining fully committed to one another.

- A husband and wife who strive to support and serve each other will rarely complain of unmet needs.
- When our hearts are right with God, our attitudes and actions will strengthen the foundation of our marriage and encourage it to become all God intended.
- Miscommunications can be avoided if we seek first to understand and second to be understood.
- No one has more potential for meeting our marital needs than our own husband or wife.
- If our spouse has wronged us, forgiving him or her will prevent bitterness and anger from eroding the foundation of our marriage.
- Husbands and wives who share the same goals and dreams are strengthening their commitment to a shared future.
- When we respond defensively, chances are that we are defending a personal weakness rather than a personal strength.
- "Love is patient, love is kind. It does not envy, it does not boast, it is not proud. It is not rude, it is not self-seeking, it is not easily angered, it keeps no record of wrongs. . . . It always protects, always trusts, always hopes, always perseveres. Love never fails" (1 Cor. 13:4–5, 7–8).

5
—

Here Today, Gone Tomorrow: Making Parenting Count

> *One of the few certainties in life is that*
> *we will look back and wish that we had*
> *spent more time enjoying our children.*
> WILLIAM L. COLEMAN

Jerry and Phyllis stood beside Michael's crib gazing in wonder at their brand-new baby son. The months of waiting were over, and the guest of honor occupied the beautifully decorated nursery at last. Jerry and Phyllis smiled at each other. They felt blessed beyond words. They were thrilled; they were fascinated—they were terrified!

It has been said that the theories of child rearing are really quite simple; it's only when we begin putting them into practice that they become difficult. Although parenting is as old as the human race, the challenges seem to grow more complicated as time goes on.

Changes in society have moved children further away from the center of our care and concern. Two-career families, the rising divorce rate, loss of extended family support, and declining values all contribute to the difficult task of raising healthy, secure children. Yet we hear messages through various media that would have us believe that parenting is a part-time endeavor that can simply be added to our plate like one more side dish at a buffet. If there was ever a need for wisdom and balance, it's in our parenting.

THE PARENT TRAP

Former President Harry S. Truman once said, "I have found the best way to give advice to your children is to find out what they want and then advise them to do it." Parenting by default may seem like the easy way at the time, but in the long run our children will suffer from our laziness, and so will we.

The "long run" is what parenting is all about. Raising children is much like running a marathon. From their very first step, we realize that the challenge before us will require endurance, determination, and training. Although it may seem easier to think of the event as a series of sprints, a sprinter is at a serious disadvantage when distance is the issue. The quick and easy solutions often take us in the opposite direction of our goal of raising godly, responsible children. Being a parent is the most important job we may ever have; our children's future depends on doing our best.

> *A baby is God's opinion that the world should go on.*
> —CARL SANDBURG

A renegade point of view has recently surfaced, which argues that parents don't play the significant role in child development we once believed. Instead, the supporters of this theory say that a child's peers have the greater impact on his morals, character, and values. Even though peers are important and influential, this argument falls apart under scrutiny. The world has changed, but parents will always carry the privilege and responsibility of being the primary influence on their children. As the old saying goes, "As the twig is bent, so grows the tree."

BENDING THE TWIG

The Bible is succinct yet profound on the subject of raising children:

> *Train a child in the way he should go,*
> *and when he is old he will not turn from it. (Prov. 22:6)*

Training a child in the way he *should* go is entirely different from the way he is *inclined* to go. A child comes into this world complete with a will that desires its own way. Proverbs 22:6 gives us both a comfort and a warning. A parent who is committed to thoughtfully training his child will be comforted; however, the parent who neglects this responsibility should be warned. We can't just close our eyes and hope our kids turn out well. Teaching scriptural values and truths when our children are young greatly increases the probability of raising a well-behaved child who will one day grow to be a responsible adult. The best time to grow straight trees and godly people is when they're young.

What we're talking about here is maintaining a perspective on our parenting role—even through the daily grind of laundry, homework, and dental appointments. We are not just striving to get through the day or even to get them through college; we are laying the groundwork for a stable and productive life.

Remember the story of the two bricklayers? When asked what he was doing, the first man answered, "I'm laying bricks and mortar." But the second man replied, "I'm building a cathedral!" Perspective lifts the mundane into the realm of the heavenly! By laying the bricks of parenting day after day, we are really striving to build independent and responsible young men and women who will love and serve God. If we are to succeed, several principles and practices must be consciously applied to our parenting.

> *When Jesus put the little child in the midst of his disciples, he did not tell the child to become like his disciples, he told the disciples to become like the little child.*
> —RUTH BELL GRAHAM

CONSISTENT DISCIPLINE

Some years ago, a research study was conducted to discover how children on a playground would respond when the perimeter fence was removed. When the fence was there the children used every inch of the playground to run, kick balls, play tag and hide-and-seek. Afterwards, however, the children confined their play to a very small area of grass near the school building. Without the clearly defined boundary of the fence, they no longer had a clear understanding of where they could safely play. Setting well-defined limits is not punitive; children crave the structure and security.

Without limits, children can't learn the difference between right and wrong behavior. Determining boundaries is also a fundamental step to establishing discipline. When a child knows the rules and the consequences of breaking them, power struggles and misunderstandings decrease, while cooperation increases.

Many parents are great at establishing rules, but when it comes to following through with them, they miss the mark. Inconsistent discipline opens the door to weakened authority and ultimately, a lack of respect. When children choose to step outside the established boundaries, they need to know that consequences will follow.

Rules—even good rules—are not enough. Author and teen advocate Josh McDowell often says that rules without a relationship will lead to rebellion. A parent who spends time with his child will have the opportunity to listen and understand him. In this relaxed atmosphere, instruction and rules are comfortably sandwiched between conversation, laughter, and activity.

> *Fathers, do not provoke your children to*
> *anger; but bring them up in the discipline*
> *and instruction of the Lord. (Eph. 6:4 NASB)*

This kind of interaction builds strong and trusting relationships. Rules are just restrictions unless a child knows they have been set out of love and concern.

Even though consistency is essential to maintaining discipline, there will be times when rules should give way to grace. After all, were it not for God's grace, we would all be in serious trouble! God has shown every believer the great gift of unmerited love and favor. We didn't do a thing to earn it, but he lavished it upon us.

> My mother had a
> great deal of trouble
> with me, but I think
> she enjoyed it.
> —MARK TWAIN

In its ancient Hebrew *grace* means "to stoop" or "to bend." If we are parenting with grace, we should frequently allow ourselves to stoop to our children's level so that we can connect with them in their world. And when we bend to demonstrate our pure love and acceptance of them regardless of whether they are being good or bad, they learn that nothing feels quite so wonderful as gracious love.

GODLY INSTRUCTION

A parent may love his child immeasurably but unintentionally teach her harmful attitudes. As vital as love is, in the absence of instruction, a child will be undisciplined and lacking in self-control and respect for others. Scripture tells us when we put God first, guidance and godly instruction will flow out of the simplest situations.

> *Fix these words of mine in your hearts and minds . . .*
> *Teach them to your children, talking about them when*
> *you sit at home and when you walk along the road, when*
> *you lie down and when you get up. (Deut. 11:18–19)*

When our faith is deeply woven into the fabric of our life, our children grow up knowing that God is for every waking minute, not just a Sunday morning ritual. Regardless of how much we talk to our kids about Jesus, the strongest statements come when our actions match our words. Then the lessons become a vibrant reality before our children's eyes. If we catch ourselves saying, "Do as I say, not as I do," we can be certain that we must first learn the lesson ourselves before our kids will take it to heart.

The best inheritance a father can leave his children is a good example.
—UNKNOWN

In our current times it's more important than ever for the home to be the primary place for learning basic values and morals. Only a few decades ago, parents could count on society to reinforce basic standards of moral behavior. No longer. Now, when our kids go to school, they are constantly exposed to teachings and attitudes contrary to those found in the Bible. They hear that truth is a relative matter and respect for others means unquestioning acceptance of all beliefs and opinions. Judging another's choices and actions is viewed as a sign of prejudice and intolerance.

Therefore, it's up to Christian parents to teach their children fundamental godly truths: Every human being is a unique creation of God; the most important things in life can't be bought; choices have consequences; and there are absolute truths and a reliable standard of right and wrong—the Bible. This is a mighty tall order in our permissive and misled times. The rewards, however, are great if our children know the ways of the Lord and live moral lives.

LOVE, LOVE, LOVE

Love is the magic ingredient that underlies mental health and plays a vital role in physical health as well. The relationship between parent and child should be modeled after God's relationship with man.

> *My command is this: Love each other*
> *as I have loved you. (John 15:12)*

Most parents would probably feel that it is unnecessary to be reminded to love their children. Yet the command to love with the same love with which Christ has loved us far exceeds our natural capability. Therefore, our goal is not only to love and be loved by our children but also to help root them in the imperishable love of Christ. Our prayer for them should echo Paul's prayer for the Ephesians when he prayed that Christ would dwell in their hearts through faith.

> *And I pray that you, being rooted and established in love,*
> *may have power, together with all the saints, to grasp how*
> *wide and long and high and deep is the love of Christ,*
> *and to know this love that surpasses knowledge—that you may*
> *be filled to the measure of all the fullness of God. (Eph. 3:17–19)*

To demonstrate unconditional love to our children, we must point them to Jesus. Yes, it's important that we do our best to love them unconditionally, as well, but we are human; God is God. When we launch our children into the world, the path is littered with peril. An empty heart that has yet to know love will risk almost any danger to fill it. Loving God equips children to function in a fickle and parched world. Friends may be betray them, love relationships may suddenly end, but when their roots are nourished by the living water of Jesus, they will survive.

LETTING GO

The last piece of furniture was loaded onto the moving van, and the metal door slammed shut. Jerry and Phyllis stood in the empty living room and held each other close. The late-afternoon sun streamed through the windows and sprawled across the gleaming wood floors. Memories seemed to ricochet off the bare surfaces. Wasn't it just yesterday that they brought Michael home from the hospital and placed him in his crib? Emily and Amy had followed shortly thereafter. Now the kids were all grown up. Could it all be over so soon?

As quickly as the child-rearing phase seems to pass, the parental work is not entirely done. In fact, one of the most important phases of parenting has just begun: letting go—while gently holding on. This can prove to be a new form of coordination for parents—something like patting one's head while rubbing the tummy. Yet adult relationships with our kids and their families are some of the parent's sweetest rewards.

As the following stories reveal, successful parenting is an ongoing process of learning and a vital partnership with our heavenly Father.

> *Life with Christ is endless love; without him it is a loveless end.*
> —BILLY GRAHAM

THE CHANGE OF HEART

When Trina came back into their lives, Linda and David were less than thrilled. The family had known Trina for years through the youth group at their church. Instead of going to college or pursuing a career after high school, she had moved to another city and become pregnant by the boy she was living with. Now, four months along, she had already broken up with the boyfriend and moved back to town. To their great distress, it looked as though she and their youngest son, Tim, were dating and becoming serious.

"Honey, think about what you're getting yourself into!" Linda pleaded with Tim. "What if the father of that baby decides at some point that he wants to be involved? Your life will be so complicated; you don't deserve that."

Linda and David had high hopes for their two sons. Having finished only two years of college themselves, they placed a premium on education. Todd, their older son, had not disappointed them. He had finished college before marrying a lovely Christian girl from a good family. She had finished her undergraduate degree with honors and was already pursuing a master's.

Why would they want any less in a bride for Tim? After all, he was an exceptional young man who brimmed with potential. In his junior year of college, he was an athlete who also excelled academically. He had every reason to face the future with unhindered optimism. They pictured him eventually married to a well-educated girl from a stable, Christian home.

Although Tim and Trina had met through their church youth group when they were both in high school, Trina had come from a troubled family. Her father was not around, and her mother struggled with drug addiction. Things had gotten so bad at home that Trina's grandparents had taken her in. The adversity in her young life manifested in many ways, not the least of which was in relationships with boys that got too close too fast.

In Linda's mind Trina didn't even begin to meet her expectations for a wife for her son. She was determined to do everything in her power to prevent their relationship from progressing.

Toward that end Linda and David refused to acknowledge that there was any commitment between Trina and Tim. Even when Trina was present, they encouraged their son to date other people. "You're young, Tim," they told him. "You shouldn't be going steady with anyone right now; you should date several different girls." Trina's gaze would drop to the floor, but she said and did nothing.

When she was not around, Linda and David were even more blunt and discouraging. "What makes you think Trina will be faithful to you? Just look at her past!" Linda said. David was quick to point out that Trina's lack of education could eventually be a problem that would make them incompatible.

Tim was steadfast in the face of their objections. "I've thought of all those things. I love Trina. I want to marry her. I just hope and pray that one day you will love her too."

Neither their son's pleas nor the fact that he and Trina were now engaged softened Linda and David. In fact, they became more determined to save Tim from making what they felt was a horrible mistake. They prayed that God would open his eyes and change his heart.

As the baby's due date approached, the constant pressure and conflict were taking a toll on Tim. One evening, he brought Trina home and said to his parents, "The four of us are going to sit down and talk this out."

The evening was a disaster despite Trina telling them how they had inspired her when she was in high school. "I used to love coming to this house. I didn't have a family like this, and I admired yours so much. I dreamed that someday I might have a family just like yours. But now I don't even feel welcome in your home."

For an instant, Linda pictured the young, hopeful high school girl who had sat on the family room floor laughing with the other kids from the youth group. The image caused an odd feeling to well in her throat. But she shook it off and continued with her barrage of objections to their plans to marry and criticisms of Trina and her pregnancy.

Trina broke her silence and said, "At least I'm having this baby! I didn't get an abortion. I'm trying to be responsible!"

"How can you call yourself responsible?" Linda shouted. "With all the birth control available, you somehow managed to get yourself pregnant!" The full force of Linda's anger was unleashed as she finally said the words that had always been implied but never spoken, "You're just not good enough for our son!"

Trina lowered her head and cried.

For weeks after that horrible evening, Linda privately thought about Trina's high school memories of their family. During these moments her anger gave way to a confusing array of emotions and sadness. Trina had admired them during those years, and now they had forcefully turned against her. As she considered this, she had to acknowledge that through it all Trina had never once lashed out at them with harsh words. Through sadness and humiliation she had been completely kind and respectful.

Yet another emotion was crowding into Linda's heart—guilt.

The birth of the baby overshadowed these thoughts with a new storm of anger and indignation. Tim had agreed to be in the delivery room with Trina. Not only did he coach her through labor; he cut the umbilical cord after the baby boy was born. Linda was livid. "Trina just robbed him of what should be an intimate experience with his own wife and child!"

Alone with Tim in the car one day, Linda resumed her efforts to persuade him to leave Trina. "Honey, Dad and I are just afraid a marriage to Trina won't last."

Tim stopped the car and turned to his mother. His eyes were filled with tears. "Mom, I can't believe I'm still hearing this! I've given Trina a ring. I love her! I want her to be my wife! This is just killing me!"

Seeing her son in such pain—pain she had caused—brought Linda to a raw and crushing realization. For the first time her thoughts turned fully to the impact of her own actions. *I'm his mother,* she thought, *yet I'm constantly hurting him when I should be supporting and loving him! I've said and done such mean things to the girl he loves. I call myself a Christian woman, but my actions have been marked by meanness, yet Trina has only shown me Jesus in everything she's said and done. And this is the young woman I've felt was not good enough for my son!*

Linda's tears began to flow carrying with them the bitterness and anger that had consumed her for months.

Although the realization was slow in coming, she quickly took the first step toward reconciliation. "Tim, I'm so sorry," she said. "I've been wrong, and I will make a vow to you right now that I'll never say another unkind or negative thing about Trina to you or to anyone else. I hope both of you will be able to forgive me."

Through much prayer and several heart-to-heart talks, healing began. Trina joyfully received Linda's efforts to repair the relationship. David was supportive of his wife's changed attitude, and in time he also grew to accept and love his new daughter-in-law.

After two years of marriage, Tim and Trina are expecting a new baby—a girl this time. Tim loves being a father to three-year-old Anthony, and the official adoption will soon be final. Although at the time she railed against it, Linda readily acknowledges that God cemented the bond of father and son early on by having Tim present and active in the delivery room during Anthony's birth.

When Linda thinks about the way she treated Trina and Tim before they were married, she still feels guilt and shame. At those times she focuses on the close relationships she has with her son and daughter-in-law now. Their love and acceptance help her feel the forgiveness she knows she has received, both from them and from God.

There's a time and a place for strong, parental influence, but there's also a time to let go and support our children in their own choices. When we are praying for God to step in and change our child's heart, we just may discover, as Linda did, that the heart God wants to change is our own.

LISTEN TO ME!

Cheryl gathered the groceries from the trunk of the car. She glanced over the tops of the bags to see that Amber had left the garden hose running—again! Water ran across the sidewalk and snaked down the gutter toward the street.

In the kitchen she set the groceries on the counter and began emptying the bags.

"Amber!" she called. "Come here this minute!"

The tone of her voice said it all. Seven-year-old Amber peeked around the corner and meekly said, "Yes, Mom?"

"You left the water on again, and now it's running down the street! How many times have I told you to turn it off when you're done using it? I wish you would listen to me!"

"Sorry," said Amber. "I'll do it right now."

Cheryl stacked cans of green beans in the pantry. She hated yelling at her child, but lately it seemed that Amber was tuning her out. It had been worse for the last couple of weeks since Michael, her husband, had been in the hospital. The strain was showing on everyone.

Throughout Michael's entire life he'd had health problems. He and Cheryl had always known that one day he would need a kidney transplant. Now that the time had come, the reality had been shocking—and frightening. The surgery had gone well enough, but then last night they learned he had a rejection-related bleeding ulcer that had required several units of blood.

Amber came back into the house just as Cheryl answered the ringing phone.

Michael's voice was shaking. "Cheryl, you need to come to the hospital right away. I'm bleeding and the doctors can't get it to stop!"

Time seemed to shift into slow motion as she hung up the phone. She needed to hurry, but she was overwhelmed by her emotions and all there was to do. She had to put away the perishables, change clothes, call Michael's parents, lock up the house.

Cheryl picked up the carton of eggs and set it back down on the counter. Her heart pounded. *Am I going to lose my husband? Is Amber going to grow up without her father?* Even as her mind raced, she couldn't seem to make her body move.

"Mommy, what's wrong?" asked Amber.

"It's Daddy," said Cheryl. "We have to go to the hospital."

Once again, she picked up the eggs and looked at them. She couldn't focus. What did she need to do next? Change her shoes? Yes—she had to change out of her old sneakers. She set down the eggs and started toward the bedroom while talking to herself.

Amber followed close behind asking questions, but Cheryl couldn't organize her thoughts well enough to answer. In the bedroom she paced between the closet and the bed, setting out clothes and hanging them up again. Amber watched as her mother grew more and more panicked. Finally, she pulled on Cheryl's hand to get her attention. "Mommy! Mommy, listen to me!"

Cheryl finally stopped and looked directly into Amber's eyes.

"Mommy, listen!" Amber said. "We have to leave it to God!"

Hearing those words, Cheryl dropped to her knees, wept, and hugged her little girl. "You're right sweetheart, that's exactly what we have to do. We have to leave it to God!" Within seconds her panic subsided, and she was able to think clearly and take care of the necessary tasks before leaving for the hospital.

Michael made it through the crisis, but over the next few years there would be other health problems—a gall bladder surgery, a second kidney transplant, another bleeding ulcer. Through these trials, the family has learned to trust God in the midst of hard circumstances.

Cheryl has changed in another way as well. As a parent, she knew it was important to teach her child to listen and obey, but since that day, she's realized how very important it is to listen to her child as well. She delights in hearing Amber's ideas, her jokes and observations. And every now and then, she's blessed to hear some profoundly wise words straight from a young and faithful heart.

HOLDING ON

Sandra shut off the engine and rolled down her window. She and Becca had been waiting in the car for Holly since school let out over thirty minutes ago. Becca was restless, impatient, and growing angrier by the minute at her older sister's tardiness.

"What is taking her so long, anyway?" said Becca. "It's so hot in this car!"

The doors to the school opened. "Here she comes," said Sandra. "Finally."

They watched as Holly strolled toward the car with a group of kids that could only be described as bizarre. The popular color choice for this crew was obviously black. For variety—light black on dark black. Judging from their faces, Sandra could only conclude that what they hadn't been able to dye they had pierced. And there, laughing in the midst of them, was her fifteen-year-old daughter, Holly.

She plopped into the backseat. "Hey," she said flatly.

Becca wasn't about to let her off that easy. "What took you so long? We've been waiting out here forever!"

"Yeah, I'm glad to see you too, Sis!" sniped Holly.

These days, a sarcastic response was always just below the surface with Holly. And Becca was a master at scratching that surface.

"You *would* be glad if you'd been cooking out here in the hot car like we've been!" countered Becca.

"Enough—both of you!" said Sandra. "We've got a long drive ahead, and we'll be late to Grandpa and Grandma's as it is."

"What's the big deal, anyway?" said Holly. "It's just the grandparents—it's not like we have dinner reservations or anything."

"It's only right to be on time when you're invited for dinner, even with family."

"I don't know why I have to go. I'd rather be with my friends."

"Are those kids your friends, Holly?" asked her mother. "What happened to Shelly and Melissa?"

"Good question! They don't have any time for me since they joined the drill team. Anyway, they're hanging with jocks now. No way I'm gonna do that!"

Sandra looked in the rearview mirror. Holly's sad face betrayed her tough words.

"Those kids you were with are weird looking," said Becca. "Why do you want to hang around with people like that?"

"I like the way they look," said Holly, "they're individuals."

"Then why do they all dress the same and do the same gross things to their faces?"

Sandra interrupted the fighting words. "Holly, is this new group of kids the reason your grades have slipped lately and the reason you've been ignoring your curfew?

"No! But I might have known you'd blame them!"

"I'm not blaming them. I hold you responsible for your own actions, but maybe they're a bad influence on you."

"I like them, and they like me! If the way they look is such a problem for you, maybe I should just go live with Dad; he's more open-minded."

Sandra's face grew hot, and she pounded the steering wheel with her palm. "Well you'll have to find him first! And what makes you think he would want you to live with him? He left us because he doesn't want the responsibility of a family!" she yelled.

"He left you! Not me—you!"

"So, where is he then?" shouted Sandra. "Like it or not, you're stuck with me, so you'd just better make the best of it!"

The atmosphere in the car was frozen. Sandra hated it when the kids pushed the buttons that propelled her into fury. She tried not to get angry, but most of the time she wasn't much better at controlling herself than the girls were. What was happening to them, anyway? She'd always thought of her girls as her best friends. They used to have fun and laugh together. She would try harder with Holly—ease up on her—try to be her friend again.

Maybe it was this desire that prompted Sandra to ignore her better judgment and allow Holly to go out on Saturday night with the new group of kids. Holly promised she'd bring her friends in the house to meet her mother and that she would be home by 11:30. But when her friends arrived, Holly slipped out the door and left.

At 2:30 in the morning, Sandra was frantic with worry. She considered calling the police, but she realized she didn't know where any of the kids lived, what they drove, or even their names. She sent up a desperate prayer, "God, please just keep her safe."

It was approaching 3:00 A.M. before she heard her daughter's key in the lock. Holly reeked of smoke and liquor, and Sandra's relief was quickly followed by a storm of anger. Holly didn't argue, maybe because she was numbed by alcohol. She sat on the sofa with her hands pressed between her knees.

Sandra raved for the better part of an hour. Finally, she said, "Maybe I should just let you experience the consequences of your own bad choices! I don't know what else I can do or say. Is that what you want? Do you want me just to let you go?"

Holly looked at her through bloodshot eyes, "That's what I want. Let me go."

Sandra threw a pillow onto the sofa. "Okay! You've got it. You're on your own!" She stomped down the hall and slammed the bedroom door behind her.

The next week was horrible. Holly came and went at all hours of the day and night. On two occasions, Sandra got calls from the school saying that she had skipped classes. The house was ruled by stony silence. Even Becca, who usually couldn't resist getting in the middle of things, was keeping a low profile by spending hours in her room in front of the television or on the phone.

After a long and sleepless weekend, Sandra was exhausted as she poured herself a cup of coffee to drink on the way to work. Her new "hands-off" philosophy with Holly was a disaster. What had she been thinking? On impulse, she walked down the hall and opened Holly's bedroom door.

The bed hadn't been slept in. A note was conspicuously propped against the pillow. Sandra's heart pounded as she read it:

Mom,

It's pretty obvious that you don't care what happens to me anymore. There's no point pretending we're a family when we're not. I've found some friends who care about me, so I've gone to live with them. *Holly*

Through her tears, Sandra phoned the police and was instructed to go downtown to file a report. As she told the officer what had happened, she could hear how foolish she had been to ever believe that letting go of her precious daughter was the right thing to do.

In the car she prayed, "God, give me another chance. I promise I'll learn how to be a better mother."

After her divorce she had stopped going to church, but now it was the first place she turned. She made an appointment with a counselor. Through the sessions that followed, she realized that just when she and her kids most needed to be anchored in Christ she had set them adrift to deal with life's problems on their own. She asked God to forgive her and help her save her family.

Eight days after Holly left, she finally called to tell her mother she was okay, but that she still wasn't coming home. When Sandra started crying, Holly said, "I'd better go," and hung up. Sandra wondered if she'd blown her only chance.

But over the next few months, the phone calls gradually increased. Surprisingly, Holly and Becca talked more than when they lived together. And slowly, Sandra and Holly began to build a fragile bridge between them. She could see that her daughter desperately needed a strong, supportive mother to guide her through a dark and dangerous world.

One day on the phone, Sandra said, "I've made some terrible mistakes as a parent, but I know it's not too late for our family. We can change. It will get better, I promise! But first you need to come back home where you belong—where you're loved. Becca misses you so much, and I do too. I love you, baby. Please, come home."

Five months after she had left, Holly came back home. It wasn't easy. Holly's initial warm feelings about being home were followed by outrage as her mother set firm limits and stuck to them. Sandra insisted that she join her in counseling. It took time for Holly to drop her barriers, but eventually they learned to talk and listen without allowing anger to rule the outcome. Sandra stopped trying to be her girls' best friend and determined to be the best parent she could be—even if it meant enduring their anger and being the "bad guy" at times.

In one session, the counselor shared the observation that success was often a simple matter of holding on after others have let go. That really hit home. Sandra had foolishly let go of Holly when her daughter had needed her the most. But, thankfully, God never let go of any of them. Raising her girls wouldn't be easy, but God would be by her side, guiding her step-by-step. She would never turn her back on one of her girls again. She would hold on—no matter what.

KEEPING WATCH

Susie bent down and tucked the covers around her sleeping daughter, Jessica. How serene she looked in sleep—and how different from the perpetual motion and endless chatter that propelled her through her days! Though not yet two years old, Jessica was the "wild child" of the house. She adored her four-month-old sister, Erin, and she constantly played with her and tried to entertain her. One of her favorite games was sneaking under Erin's crib and lying on her back while kicking the mattress or popping up at the side to squeal "peek-aboo!" Her baby sister's startled response inevitably gave way to the smiles and coos that delighted and encouraged Jessica.

In the peaceful quiet of the night, Susie stood at the doorway of their room and pondered her blessings. "Lord," she prayed, "thank you for my precious, healthy children. I can't be with them every second, but you can. Please have their guardian angels continue doing such a wonderful job keeping watch over them."

Wearily Susie shuffled down the hall to her bedroom. As much as she loved taking care of her kids, she was continually amazed by the physical demands of motherhood. Every night she sank into such a deep sleep that she could scarcely be awakened. Because of this, Greg was the one who routinely got up to do "bottle duty" during the middle of the night. She was rarely even aware when Erin cried or when Greg had left their bed to go feed her.

"Susie, check your family!" Susie's eyes flew open at the sound of an unfamiliar male voice. Had she dreamed it? Was it in her head, or had the words been spoken aloud? She didn't know. She glanced at the clock: 3:00 A.M.

Hearing her husband's rhythmic breathing assured her that he was fine. She leapt out of bed and ran down the hall to the girls' room. As she entered, she saw that Erin had wiggled into the far corner of her crib. Right before her eyes, the mattress was slowly tilting downward. Erin's head was jammed between the wooden frame of the crib and the corner of the mattress, which had wedged under her chin with a vice-like hold. It was only a matter of seconds before the full weight of her body would have tightened the pressure around her neck and strangled her.

Susie had to push the mattress down even further to release Erin's head from the jaws created by the mattress and crib frame. She carefully lifted Erin out of the crib and clutched her still-sleeping infant to her heart.

Greg could scarcely comprehend what had happened until he saw that one of the crib supports had been knocked loose—probably during one of Jessica's vigorous play sessions under the crib. Knowing what a sound sleeper Susie is, Greg solemnly agreed that it had to be the Lord who prompted her that night. They pondered the chain of remarkable events.

Sometimes the job of safely raising their children feels overwhelming. It was good to be reminded that they're not in this alone. The Lord loves their children too, and he's always there, keeping watch.

Looking Back on Lessons Learned

- Parenting isn't about raising children; it's about raising mature and productive adults.
- Like running a marathon, parenting requires a steady, consistent pace and a commitment to the long run.
- When we provide our children with clearly defined rules and limits, we are meeting a basic need for security while simultaneously letting them know they are loved.
- When a child understands the rules and the consequences for breaking them, power struggles and misunderstanding decrease while cooperation and respect increase.
- We will never get a second chance to raise our children.
- Rules are just restrictions unless a child knows they have been established out of love and concern. Without a solid relationship, rules will lead to rebellion.
- As vital as love is, it's not enough. Parental instruction will ensure a child that is disciplined, self-controlled, and respectful of others.
- As our children grow older, we must encourage them to be less dependent upon us and more dependent upon God.
- If we fail to relinquish parental power and control over our children, we will stifle God's potential impact on their lives.
- The key ingredients to successful parenting include equal measures of instruction, discipline, grace, and boundless love.
- A wise parent not only knows when to talk but also when to stop talking and listen.

- We must resist the temptation to thoughtlessly give in to our child's wants. Standing firm is one of the most effective ways of demonstrating love.
- It's inevitable that we will occasionally disagree with our spouse about how to raise our kids, but in the presence of our children we must present a unified front.
- Wise parents will not neglect the needs of their marriage in order to meet the wants of their children.

6

—

Lean on Me:
The Gift of Friendship

*There is no possession more valuable
than that of a good and faithful friend.*
SOCRATES

"Man, we're taking a beating, aren't we?" The voice came from
behind Rick as he stood in line to get a hot dog at halftime.

"You got that right!" Rick answered.

Rick had seen Charlie at almost all the football games this season
because he and his wife sat two rows in front of Rick and Connie. On
a couple of occasions they'd said hi, but this was the first time they
had ever spoken.

They introduced themselves, and Rick lingered while Charlie got
his order. Back at their seats, they introduced their wives to each
another. When the game was over, they talked again, and Charlie suggested that they make a date to meet for dinner and go to the next
game together.

That was thirty-five years ago. Charlie and Rick have been friends
ever since. Over the years they've shared countless backyard barbe-
cues, rejoiced over the births of seven children, comforted each other
at times of loss, and celebrated the marriages of their kids. Either man
would be quick to say that their friendship has been one of the greatest joys of life.

THE RISKS AND REWARDS OF REACHING OUT

Charlie's actions might have appeared impromptu, but he had
noticed Rick and Connie at previous games and had made a conscious
decision to talk with them at the first opportunity. He had a feeling

they might have a lot in common. It was risky to strike up a conversation with a virtual stranger. But when that went well, Charlie took another risk and invited Rick and Connie to dinner.

Although he wasn't the initiator of the friendship, Rick played an important role too. If he hadn't lingered at the hot dog stand and kept the conversation going, Charlie might not have extended the invitation to dinner. That brief conversation resulted in both families enjoying a lifetime of friendship. Rick and Charlie are glad they took the risk.

WHO NEEDS FRIENDS?

In a recent study a group of adults was asked if they had a same-sex best friend. The poll revealed that more than half did not, and when the statistics on men were isolated, 75 percent admitted they did not have a best friend.

Judging by these results, we might be tempted to conclude that friendships are not very important to us. However, when these same individuals were asked whether they *wanted* a best friend, the overwhelming majority answered yes.

> A friend is a gift you give yourself.
> —ROBERT LOUIS STEVENSON

It's ironic that we can be surrounded by other people yet still feel lonely. Our fast-paced society contributes to the problem by placing a high value on independence and privacy. Technological advancements such as the Internet can contribute by allowing us to become cloistered away in our homes.

Even our work scenarios have been altered by technology. "Telecommuting" via a home computer linked to the office or business is an increasingly popular work option that allows us the luxury of working at home but deprives us of the social interactions that occur in the workplace. The unexpected consequence of these technological advances is that we have to try harder than ever to cultivate friendships.

Our need for friendships has not changed through the ages. King Solomon was a wise and learned man who clearly understood the importance and benefits of friendship.

Two are better than one, because they have a good return
for their work: If one falls down, his friend can help him up.
But pity the man who falls and has no one to help him up!
Also, if two lie down together, they will keep warm.
But how can one keep warm alone? Though one may
be overpowered, two can defend themselves. A cord of
three strands is not quickly broken. (Eccles. 4:9–12)

A very practical assessment of friendship! If one falls down when he is alone, who will help him to his feet? If one were taking a beating from an enemy, what would be more welcome than another pair of strong hands to come to his aid? Bottom line: we need friends.

Yet some people are unwilling to admit they need friends. They convince themselves that it's not worth the risk; they can manage on their own. According to Solomon a friend is someone who makes you stronger, not weaker. But maybe they've been hurt in the past, and they don't want to be hurt again. Self-imposed isolation can be a trap that may be covering a deeper problem—pride.

It's not always easy to make friends. When we were kids, things were somehow simpler. We were thrown together at school or in the neighborhood, and a chain reaction of association naturally increased our circle of acquaintances. Day after day, we were around each other in uncontrived situations, and friendships grew.

As adults, however, our lives are more complicated and independent. Sometimes the mere acknowledgment that we need human connection and companionship can make us feel vulnerable. However, when we lower the barriers to our private selves, we enhance the opportunity to be known—and loved. We often fear that unless we are protective and private our weaknesses and quirks may show through. Ironically, these highly individual characteristics are often what attract others to us. When our frailties are visible, we become less intimidating and more approachable.

Our differences as well as our similarities can help us create friendships. In the Old Testament Book of 1 Samuel, we find the story of the unusual friendship between David and Jonathan. David was a lowly shepherd boy who had come to prominence after single-handedly bringing down the Philistine giant, Goliath. Jonathan was the privileged son of King Saul.

David impressed Jonathan and his father. He was a handsome young man whose behavior was ruled by his faith in God. It was obvious that the Lord was with David, and it was equally obvious that the Lord was no longer with King Saul because of his past disobedience. Selfishness led Saul to make David his ally, but Jonathan's love for David was free from selfish motives. In spite of Jonathan's position as the son and successor to the king, he regarded David as his equal, and he was selflessly willing to help David.

> *Friendship is one of the sweetest joys of life. Many might have failed beneath the bitterness of their trial had they not found a friend.*
> —CHARLES H. SPURGEON

Soon King Saul's admiration of David turned to murderous jealousy. Saul became so intent on killing David that Jonathan had to help him run for his life. Jonathan was caught between his father and his friend. David and Jonathan wept as they parted, but they knew their friendship—rooted in the Lord—would always live.

Jonathan said to David, *"Go in peace, for we have sworn friendship with each other in the name of the* Lord, *saying, 'The* Lord *is witness between you and me, and between your descendants and my descendants forever.'"* (1 Sam. 20:42)

Theirs was a friendship that would not only survive trials, separations, and hardships; it would reach through the generations to eternity.

The Gifts of Friendship

In spite of the unusual obstacles to their friendship, Jonathan and David were both the richer for it. Fortunately, most of our friendships are far less complicated, and we are wonderfully flattered by the gift of being chosen to be a friend. Unlike family relationships, friendships are free of the complexities that often surround family ties. There are no expectations to live up to or to live down; we are seen with uncluttered eyes. When we are known and loved by pure choice, we experience the joy of being accepted solely for who we are.

A caring friend can encourage us to reach our dreams and support us through the tough times. While this support is wonderful, a true friend will also hold us accountable for our actions and confront us if we're headed in a wrong direction.

It's easy to "be there" for someone during the good times, but what if being a friend meant sacrifice rather than pleasure? Life can dish out pain and disappointment, but good friends can make the trials more tolerable. The Old Testament story of Ruth and Naomi is a wonderful illustration of the commitment of friendship.

Ruth was the widow of Naomi's son. Without Mahlon as their mutual tie, the two women were no longer bound to each other. Naomi knew this and encouraged her daughter-in-law to go her own way and find a husband who would make her future secure. As for herself, Naomi had decided to leave Moab and return to Judah. Ruth was aware that hardships surely lay ahead for two women without the shelter of a man, but she chose to go with Naomi.

> *I expect to pass through life but once. If, therefore, there be any kindness I can show, or any good thing I can do to any fellow being, let me do it now, for I shall not pass this way again.*
> —WILLIAM PENN

"*Where you go I will go, and where you stay I will stay.*
Your people will be my people and your God my God.
Where you die I will die, and there I will be buried.
May the Lord deal with me, be it ever so severely, if anything but death separates you and me." (Ruth 1:16–17)

These words so beautifully express complete and pure commitment that they have been repeated in many wedding ceremonies through the ages. God honored Ruth's selfless commitment and obedience to his law. He divinely opened the door to blessings for Ruth and for Naomi as well.

CHOOSE WELL

Ruth knew that Naomi was a woman of character and integrity, and Naomi knew the same of Ruth. Therefore, the commitment between them was wise and well founded. Choosing good friends requires wisdom. First Corinthians 15:33 tells us that "bad company corrupts good character." Therefore, a poor choice in a companion will not only deprive us of the joys of friendship; it can ultimately rob us of our own good character.

How can we know in advance whether a potential friend is worthy of our commitment? In the Book of Proverbs we are told the traits in a person that the Lord detests.

> There are six things the LORD hates, seven that are
> detestable to him: haughty eyes, a lying tongue, hands
> that shed innocent blood, a heart that devises wicked
> schemes, feet that are quick to rush into evil,
> a false witness who pours out lies and a man who
> stirs up dissension among brothers. (Prov. 6:16–19)

Pride, lying, murder, a person who plots evil, a person who loves to be in the midst of perverse activities, lying under oath, and causing division among believers—God hates these characteristics and actions. It's evident that these traits describe an ungodly individual. Since the Bible clearly tells us not to be yoked with unbelievers in marriage, we should apply this wise counsel and not commit ourselves to ungodly people in other relationships, either. If we ignore this advice, we will find ourselves emotionally drained and treading a downhill path.

> He who walks with the wise grows wise,
> but a companion of fools suffers harm. (Prov. 13:20)

Unfortunately, we sometimes learn these lessons the hard way because we have chosen to associate with someone with arrogant or destructive attitudes. God still loves these people, and we should lift them up in prayer, but they are poor choices to fill the important role of friend in our life.

THE ULTIMATE FRIEND

Even when we've done our best to choose good friends, we may still experience times of painful rejection. It can hurt even more when we have invested time and energy and have revealed our "real self." If a friend has wounded us, it's a natural tendency to construct a protective shield, insulate our emotions, and vow never to be vulnerable again. This strategy may remove the threat of rejection, but at the high cost of loneliness and the loss of the potential rewards of another friendship.

We may be hurting so intensely that we feel no one could understand the extent of our wounds. Jesus can. No one has ever experienced the rejection that he did. The hatred against him was so profound that it ultimately led to his execution on the cross. Not only was he rejected by the religious leadership; he was rejected and abandoned by his closest friends at the time of his greatest need.

> *Friend, you can trust that Man that died for you.*
> —JAMES M^cCONKEY

In spite of the failures and frailties of his friends, Jesus highly valued friendships. His earthly ministry began by assembling a small group of people who would learn from him and share life's trials and joys. Over the course of his ministry, this group of people became much more to Jesus than his disciples.

"I no longer call you servants, because a servant does not know his master's business. Instead, I have called you friends, for everything that I learned from my Father I have made known to you. You did not choose me, but I chose you."
(John 15:15–16)

A servant-master relationship is limited. The servant follows the directives of the master, but he is not taken into his master's confidence or allowed to share in his hopes or plans for the future. In the beginning, the disciples followed Jesus, but their relationship deepened as they spent time together, listening to his teachings and hearing his plan for mankind. They suffered rejection on his account; they witnessed his miracles and felt his incomprehensible love—they were his friends.

The friends Jesus had loved and led were conspicuously absent at the cross. Weakness and fear for their own safety were exposed under the pressure of persecution. Maybe as they huddled behind locked doors, his words swam through their minds:

"My command is this: Love each other as I have loved you. Greater love has no one than this, that one lay down his life for his friends." (John 15:12–13)

His love for his friends—and for us—took him to the cross, but most of his friends abandoned him. Could he have expressed his love for his friends more dramatically—more completely?

When we have accepted this incredible gift, we have made a Friend who will never fail us. When we are lonely, he is present; when we are maligned, he knows the truth; when we are ill, he offers hope; when we are lost, he shows us the way. He promises: "Never will I leave you; never will I forsake you" (Heb. 13:5).

Never. What an awesome Friend!

ANGIE'S ANGEL

Angie's reputation arrived at the orphanage several days before she did.

"She's going to be a handful, isn't she?" Helen, the housemother, flipped through the pages of Angie's voluminous file. "What a life! Poor little thing! Her birth father is in prison, and her birth mother abandoned her when Angie was a year old and her brother was only six! When a neighbor discovered that the children were alone in the house, she contacted the authorities."

"That just scratches the surface!" said the caseworker. "She's been in two foster homes over the last five years, and both of the foster fathers died while she was living with them."

Helen shook her head. "It's no wonder she's so angry and acting out. The world must seem like a very cruel place."

Angie turned six on the day she arrived at the orphanage. Sympathy for her tumultuous life soon gave way to exhausted frustration. Angie started fights, stole food from the kitchen, sneaked out the windows, and purposely clogged the toilets with mounds of tissues. In the first two weeks, she had five different roommates. She couldn't—or wouldn't—get along with anyone.

It didn't help that Angie always looked as though she'd just tumbled out of bed. Barrettes slipped right out of her limp brown hair, and a corner of her blouse constantly defied the waistband of her skirt. Her nose was red and peeling from a persistent cold.

Eventually Angie settled in. She realized that her mother would never come for her, and she accepted that the orphanage was her home. But at age eleven, she was still a lonely, hurting child.

At church one day Helen pointed out Angie to Carolyn, a friend of hers from Sunday school. "It just breaks my heart," said Helen. "I've never see a child that needed a friend so much."

Angie shifted her weight from one foot to the other as she read the poster on the bulletin board that announced the Valentine's Day Mother-Daughter Banquet. Carolyn studied her and smiled, thinking, *My goodness! She's all knees and elbows! She looks like a brand-new colt trying to find its balance.* "Helen, do you think she'd like to go with me to the banquet?"

Helen's face seemed to light from within. "You'll never know unless you ask!"

Angie responded with sullen suspicion. "Why would you want to go with me?" Her gaze bounced off the floor, the ceiling—anywhere but at Carolyn.

Carolyn reached for Angie's hands and waited until she was looking in her eyes. "Well, you see, angel, all my friends are married and have children of their own. So I sometimes feel lonely and left out. I would really appreciate it if you would go with me."

After the banquet Angie expected that she would never see Carolyn again, but every few days the phone would ring and Carolyn's bright voice would say, "Hi, angel! How are you doing? Let's plan something fun for the weekend."

So began the friendship that would change Angie's life. In those days single women couldn't adopt children, but Carolyn did the next best thing—she gave her time and love. In addition to taking her to Sunday school every week, she took her shopping, to museums, the zoo, and, once, to the opera. She always managed to find just the perfect gift for her birthday or Christmas. Every few months Angie sat cross-legged on Carolyn's kitchen table as Carolyn folded rectangles of tissue paper over the ends of her straight hair and wound them up on tiny rods. Angie hated the smell of the permanent waving lotion, but when it was done, she twirled through the house with curls flying. Carolyn would brush out her hair and lift Angie's chin and smile. "You look beautiful, angel!" she would say. "Those curls are the perfect frame for a lovely face."

When Angie was eighteen, she left the orphanage and moved out of state to be with her brother. She and Carolyn wrote letters and visited whenever they could. Angie missed the dear woman who had seen a lonely little orphan girl and taken her under her wings. Wings. Carolyn had always called her an angel, but it was pretty clear that

Carolyn was really the angel—sent by God himself to teach Angie how to love and be loved.

E-FRIENDS

The green numbers from the clock cast an eerie glow over the dark bedroom. Rhonda avoided looking at the time; it would only make the hours drag even slower until morning. Daniel slept peacefully beside her—both to her relief and consternation. The cold medicine probably had something to do with it. Both she and Daniel had colds, and now the baby seemed like she was getting sick, too.

In the darkness the moving boxes stacked in the corner took on a ghostly, monstrous form. Indeed, they were haunting her. The entire house was a mess. They had moved in over two weeks ago, but somehow she just couldn't summon the energy to finish unpacking. The task had taken on Everest proportions. It was their third major move in as many years. *I should be happy,* she thought. Daniel was unstoppable in his work lately; they couldn't seem to promote him fast enough. Rhonda was proud and happy for his accomplishments, but privately she admitted that she sometimes felt envious and jealous.

The moment the thought crossed her mind, she felt guilty. All her life she had wanted to be a wife and mother. Now she was both, and most of the time lately she was miserable. She'd had no idea she would miss her job at the bank so much. She missed the challenge, the orderly routines, the acknowledgment, and earning her own paycheck. In contrast, the twenty-four-hour job of motherhood left her feeling like her individual identity was lost under the stubborn layer of "baby fat" that wouldn't budge no matter how she tried.

Over the baby monitor she could hear Cassie coughing and squirming in her crib.

Rhonda pulled on her robe and stepped into her slippers. As she trudged from the bedroom, she glanced at the clock—2:17 A.M.—ugh!

Despite her stuffy nose, seven-month-old Cassie smiled and wiggled with delight when she saw Rhonda. She was such a precious baby girl; Rhonda felt guilty for her resentful thoughts. Guilt! Lately she always felt guilty about something. She fed Cassie and rocked her back to sleep.

Rhonda went into the family room and turned on a light. It was in chaos like the rest of the house, but one corner of the room stood out in completion and order. Daniel had set up the computer on the very first day. "You need to stay in touch with your on-line friends," he had said. *Bless his heart!* thought Rhonda. She feathered her fingers over the keyboard. Right now she didn't feel like she had anything to offer anyone.

After their last move Rhonda discovered a Christian Web site on the Internet. One day she read that a new E-mail loop was starting, so she signed up. At first it was just a few women, but it quickly grew to almost thirty. Through the "loop," everyone could read each E-mail, but it was strictly up to the individual whether or not to actively participate in the conversation.

Over the months, Rhonda got to know the women through their E-mails. Their various writing styles seemed to take on individual pitch and intonation—as though their voices were carried along on their words. While there were a variety of ages and professions, most were like Rhonda: stay-at-home moms. Some days they were her only adult contacts other than Daniel. It was wonderfully convenient to be able to visit with a group of women without having to dress, put on makeup, or drive somewhere. Often when Cassie went down for her nap, Rhonda made a beeline for the computer. It was more than simple conversation; Rhonda loved having the benefit of the collective wisdom and experience the group offered. It seemed that no matter what the parenting problem, someone else had "been there" and had words of advice. When someone had times of trouble, the group rallied in prayer and encouragement.

Unlike herself, some of the women had *real* problems like a husband out of work, a child with chronic illness, or an aging parent to care for. In comparison her problems sounded like someone "crying with cake in both hands" as her father would say.

She sat down and clicked onto the Internet and listened to the grindings and moanings of the modem as it dialed in and connected. The little yellow flag on her mailbox popped up, announcing, "You've got mail!"

She must have read for forty-five minutes. She learned that Claire's husband had finally found a job; Denise's two-year-old used the potty-chair for the first time; Alisa's mother was still in the hospital following a stroke; and Robin, mother of a four-month-old, was expecting again!

The last message was from Kate:

"Rhonda, where are you? Are you moved into your new home and settled yet? Didn't you remember what we told you about keeping your priorities straight—unpack the computer even before the peanut butter! Let us know you're okay."

Rhonda smiled. Maybe she'd just write a quick note to tell them she was fine but that she wouldn't be able to write again for a few weeks. She clicked on the "Reply to All" button and started typing:

Hello, Kate and friends,

Yes, we are technically moved in. Are we settled? Not even close. I write this in the wee hours of the morning. Sleep eludes me once again tonight. What I don't accomplish during the day pesters me through the night. There are mountains of unpacked boxes everywhere I look. No matter what I contemplate doing, any small obstacle completely derails my plans: Shall I put away the dishes? Then I remember that I need to line the shelves, and I have no shelf paper. Should I go to the store? But then I realize I still don't really remember where the store is.

I feel positively paralyzed when I consider all that I need to do—find a bank, a family doctor, a pediatrician, and a church. Didn't I just do all this a few months ago? I know I should be happy. I have a great husband and a darling baby girl, and somewhere under all these stupid boxes, I think I have a nice home. But really, what I want more than anything right now is to curl up on my bed, sleep for about three days, and wake up by myself on a desert island where no one can find me.

Through bleary eyes Rhonda pointed the arrow at the "Send" button and clicked.

"Oh, my gosh! What have I done?"

She instantly felt remorse. How could she let her feelings show so blatantly? Wasn't there a way to "unsend" an E-mail? But before she could figure it out, an "instant message" popped up on her screen indicating someone was on her computer at this very moment and trying to contact her. The message read:

"Rhonda, it's Kate. Are you there?"

Rhonda grimaced and typed, "Hi, Kate. I thought I was the only one in the world awake at this hour. Sorry about my self-pitying E-mail.

"Don't apologize, Rhonda. It's how you feel. You've just had a baby, you're tired from the move, and it sounds like you're pretty depressed."

"I know I shouldn't be; other people have such serious problems."

"Rhonda, depression *is* a serious problem. It's nothing to be ashamed of or feel guilty about. Now, let me ask you something—no guilt allowed—have you unpacked your Bible yet?"

"No, not yet."

"Okay. In the morning, after breakfast, make that your first priority of the day. Get back in God's Word on a daily basis, and get back on-line with your friends! Let us support you and pray for you through this time; we care about you. Don't let your pride deprive you of what you need or deprive us of the joy of ministering to you."

Through her tears Rhonda typed, "Thank you, Kate."

Kate continued. "Before I sign off, let me pass on something to you that I was reading earlier tonight:

'I will lift up my eyes to the hills—where does my help
come from? My help comes from the LORD, the Maker of
heaven and earth. He will not let your foot slip—he who
watches over you will not slumber; indeed, he who
watches over Israel will neither slumber or sleep.'

"Now, go back to bed and go to sleep, Rhonda. Rest easy because the Lord is awake. Things will get better—you'll see."

In retrospect, Rhonda could see that sharing her problems with other people has always been hard for her. But maybe that's why her Internet friendships are so special. There's a measure of safety in opening up to this immensely important but largely anonymous group of women. Over the next few days, Rhonda's E-mail overflowed with Scriptures and encouragement. Women from all over the country assured her that they understood what she was going through and that they were praying for her.

Kate was right. Little by little things began to fall into place. She and Daniel found a good church that has a wonderful women's Bible study group. It was great to make new friends. As wonderful as her Internet buddies are, nothing beats a face-to-face hug. She still checks in daily with her E-mail loop, and she thanks God for providing such a wonderful group of friends who were there for her at the perfect time—on-line.

ALL THINGS POSSIBLE

"Let's take a short motorcycle ride before dinner, okay?" John slipped on his helmet and handed the other one to his wife.

"It'll have to be a short one; the kids will be hungry soon," Karen said as she fastened the strap snugly beneath her chin.

It was late afternoon on a July day in 1999. As they pulled onto the road, the breeze felt wonderful on John's face. But less than a quarter of a mile from their home, their pleasure ride turned tragic. A Suburban truck veered in front of them so suddenly that John didn't have an instant to take evasive measures. The motorcycle crashed into the side of the truck. Although no one in the Suburban was hurt, John took the full impact of the collision. He was thrown thirty feet from the point of impact, leaving impressions in the door panel where his arms, legs, and face had hit. His body cushioned Karen to some extent, but she was rendered unconscious and lay in the middle of the road. John was conscious but close to death. In addition to a host of minor injuries, his skull was fractured in several places, his jaw crushed, both eyes were damaged, and his nose was torn from his face.

It would have been easy to believe that his life had suddenly spun out of control, but as John looks back on it, he sees that God was there every minute through the doctors and through family. For this reason, he refers to the events of that day as the "crash" rather than the "accident" because with God there are no accidents, only events that he allows to occur in our lives to accomplish his purposes. One very evident purpose was to demonstrate God's love and care through the actions of their believing friends.

John and Karen are part of a small group of seven couples who meet for Bible study and prayer on a regular basis. Word traveled so quickly among these friends that some of them actually arrived at the University Medical Center before the ambulance. John and Karen's two sons came to the hospital with the officers that had been at the scene. Unfortunately, that meant that they saw John with his face crushed and struggling to stay alive. It was a traumatic picture they can't erase from their minds—a picture that still causes them pain.

Karen's injuries were not as dramatic as John's, but even so, on three occasions her blood pressure dropped so low that the doctors thought they might lose her. Miraculously, however, she was able to go home after only four days in the hospital.

John, however, was in the Intensive Care Unit for almost two weeks and in a regular room for two weeks more. From the very beginning, a friend or family member was with him almost twenty-four hours a day. Often it was someone either from their small group or the church choir. If they weren't with John in the hospital, they were at their home, helping Karen and the kids, providing meals, or even cleaning the house. John's parents were also on the scene as constant sources of support and help.

Almost immediately John and Karen's situation was lifted up through prayer chains around the world and over E-mail. Through the ordeal they received over five hundred cards and countless E-mails. Because John is a part of a radio ministry, he got cards and letters from listeners across the country.

People sent tapes and CDs for him to listen to—a particular blessing as his left eye was bandaged, his right eye was blind, and he couldn't talk because his jaw had been surgically reconstructed and wired shut. All he had was his hearing. He listened to praise-and-worship music filled with Scripture. Although heavily sedated with morphine, he still remembers hearing those life-giving words. They reassured him that God was in control and looking out for him and for the welfare of his wife and children.

Along the way there were some dramatic answers to prayer. At first the doctors thought John would be blind. His left eye had ruptured, and the injuries were so extensive that the doctors felt it needed to be removed. When their friends learned this, they began praying for healing and restoration of his sight. Although it was a long shot, a team of doctors performed an eight-hour surgery, which saved John's eye and eventually restored the vision to 20/20.

Friends also tended to mundane but important tasks. One good friend, Becky, was nothing short of an angel to John. With severe head trauma comes swelling of the brain and the inability of the body to regulate its temperature. As a result, he sweated profusely, often soaking his hospital gown. Becky found where the gowns were kept and maintained a supply of them in his room. Whoever was with John through the night sometimes changed his gown up to five times. It seems like a small thing, but it made a huge difference in his comfort.

Two other friends provided unique comfort as well. John's former pastor, John Losen and his son, John Jr., have known John since1970. When they heard what had happened, they immediately flew out from Michigan. John Jr. left his business to stay with John for two weeks after the crash—often taking care of him during the difficult overnight shift. John's condition was especially volatile during those first two weeks. His face was raw and swollen, and the plastic surgeries that would eventually reconstruct his nose had not yet been done. To make matters worse, the medications caused episodes of hallucinations and aggressive behavior. Although John neither looked nor acted the same, his friends cared for him and graciously overlooked everything else.

The presence of his friends not only provided the comforting knowledge that he was not alone; it also had a profound impact on his physical healing. Because his jaw was wired shut, he was fed protein drinks by a syringe inserted between a gap in his teeth. He had no appetite, but John Jr. quietly forced him to eat. The nutrition helped maintain his strength and prevented what could have been a major setback in his recovery.

After a month in the hospital, John was transported to a rehabilitation hospital. Doctors told him that he would have to be there for quite a while, but his quick progress enabled his release after only a week and a half. Yet even after returning home, he had a long way to go. His jaw was still wired shut, so he had to use a respiratory aid. He was almost blind. He had a trach tube in his throat to aid his breathing since he couldn't yet breathe through his nose. It was an excruciating and humbling time.

This incredible trial has reset and strengthened John's priorities. He now has a recommitted passion for a closer walk with Jesus and a desire to be there for his wife and their kids. Other things have changed, too. Before the crash, little things used to ruffle his feathers, but now not nearly so much. Simple joys like taking a walk with Karen, having a family meal, or just looking at the mountains and feeling the sun on his face have taken on new meaning and value.

Four months after the crash, Karen and John flew back to Michigan to visit friends and family. John Jr. picked them up at the airport around midnight. It was the first time they'd seen each other since those first long and gruesome weeks in the hospital.

They were headed down the freeway toward Ann Arbor when John Jr. turned up the volume on the radio. "Wait a second, wait a second!" he said.

It was one of the songs they had listened to repeatedly in the hospital called "Shout to the Lord"—a song about how praiseworthy God is, and that all things are possible through Christ.

"This is our theme song," he said. He reached over and grabbed John's hand.

From the back seat Karen caught a glimpse of John Jr. as headlights lit his face. He was smiling and singing at the top of his lungs as tears ran down his face.

What an incredible friend!

All of their friends were right there to reach out to them during their time of great need. Not only did their friends have a profound effect on their healing but also, John believes, on their survival. John thought they were close before, but now there's an even stronger bond, and John and Karen love them in a whole new way.

It was an ordeal John wouldn't wish on anyone, but it came with surprising blessings and joys. In the midst of such hardships, that might seem impossible, but with God all things are possible.

- Friendships require an element of risk, but the rewards can last a lifetime.
- A good friend will graciously overlook our flaws and focus on our strengths.
- Corrupt friends lead us down a path of destruction, while friends of good character encourage us to be the best we can be.
- To make a friend we must be friendly; to keep a friend we must give of ourselves.
- A true friend will alert us when we are in danger of compromising our values and morals.
- Tennyson's line is still true: "'Tis better to have loved and lost than never to have loved at all."
- We all have times when we fall. We are truly blessed when we have a friend to help us up. Reliance on a friend is not a sign of weakness but evidence of wisdom and strength.
- During times of grief and sorrow, a friend's worth is never more evident. God often uses our friendships as a tonic for our emotional pain.
- Time with friends makes our lives more balanced. We must choose our friends carefully because they influence us greatly.
- Friendship has a greater chance for success when we concentrate on what we can give to the relationship rather than what we can get from it.
- A close friendship is defined by two people who are so secure in their relationship that they are not afraid to be transparent and vulnerable with one another.
- A friendship between believers is an eternal friendship.
- Unfortunately, sometimes even our friends can let us down, but God is a Friend who will never fail us.

7

Nine to Five

*Whatever your hand finds to do, do it
with all your might, for in the grave, where
you are going, there is neither working
nor planning nor knowledge nor wisdom.*
ECCLESIASTES 9:10

*I*t seemed as though Bill had just laid his head on the pillow when the
alarm rang. He reached for the buzzer and thought, *How can the
nights go so fast when the workdays go so slow?* He shuffled to the bathroom and stared into the mirror. His reflection looked back at him
with a scowl that revealed his attitude. *I hate Mondays—and
Tuesdays—and Wednesdays…I hate my job!*

Bill had worked as an insurance salesman for sixteen years.
Although he'd never been exactly *happy* with his job, his good performance was rewarded and he was promoted to district sales manager. It was now Bill's responsibility to train and manage a sales force
of fifty men and women over four states, and he hated his job.

Ironically, for years Bill thought he would enjoy work if only he
was in management. Now that he was there, he found out that the
position came with unanticipated frustrations and pressures. While
the idea of training people sounded enjoyable and satisfying, Bill soon
discovered that he was impatient and poorly equipped to explain to
others what he so thoroughly understood himself.

Concealing his frustrations had become an exercise in self-control.
One afternoon, however, his patience snapped. As he explained the
fourth quarter sales figures for the third time to a trainee, Bill watched
the man's brow furrow in bewilderment yet again.

Bill threw down his pencil. "For heaven's sake," he said, "this isn't rocket science! Are you even trying, or are you just stupid?"

The young man's face seemed to collapse in embarrassment and indignation.

Bill was horrified at his own words and apologized immediately. "I'm sorry," he said. "That was totally uncalled for."

The trainee mildly accepted his apology, but a coworker alerted Bill's supervisor to the incident. Before he knew it, Bill was sitting across the desk from his boss discussing his difficulties in effectively handling the stresses of his new job.

ARE WE AT WAR WITH WORK?

Bill is not alone in his negative feelings about work. A recent survey revealed that between 60 and 70 percent of all working Americans would change jobs if given the opportunity. This is a significant change from only a generation ago when long-term employment and company loyalty were more the norm. Now it's not uncommon for a person to have up to five different careers during his or her working lifetime. This can be disconcerting for those who crave security, but it can also be exciting and liberating.

> There is no future in any job. The future lies in the man who holds the job.
> —GEORGE CRANE

Over the course of a lifetime, the average person will spend almost half of his or her waking hours on the job. That's more than 11,700 days or 93,600 hours! Whether a stockbroker on Wall Street or a stock clerk in a hardware store, our quality of life will be defined, in large part, by the satisfaction we derive from work. And our satisfaction will depend greatly on the work we choose and the day-to-day decisions we make while on the job.

Work has been around since the creation of man. In Genesis 2:15 we read that "the LORD God took man and put him in the Garden of Eden to work it and take care of it." From the beginning it was necessary for man to cultivate and protect the land in order to ensure its productivity. The more attention and care given to the land the more it yielded.

We can apply this principle to our work today. Working with thoughtful attention and care will likely result in greater productivity, competence, satisfaction, and I hope, a bigger paycheck.

Unfortunately, many people don't experience these positive results and tend to view work as a necessary evil. Holding a job becomes a burden they bear to put food on the table and a roof overhead. This negative mind-set can dominate our thoughts to the extent that we don't even try to take steps to improve or change things. We give up.

King Solomon may have been one of the first men to commit his work frustrations to paper.

> *So I hated life, because the work that is done under*
> *the sun was grievous to me. All of it is meaningless,*
> *a chasing after the wind. (Eccles. 2:17)*
> *What does a man get for all the toil and anxious striving*
> *with which he labors under the sun? All his days his*
> *work is pain and grief; even at night his mind does not rest.*
> *This too is meaningless. (Eccles. 2:22–23)*

It is obvious that Solomon was grappling with larger issues than the significance of work; he was searching for the meaning of his life on earth. He had become bitter and depressed because nothing he had pursued filled his emptiness. As he contemplated his future, he could see the possibility of working diligently and gradually accumulating wealth, only to die and have it fall into the hands of someone who never worked a day for it. He anticipated an endless cycle of working every day only to worry through the night. No wonder he was depressed!

At this point Solomon's perspective was totally earthbound. He was looking solely to his work to provide satisfaction and purpose in his existence. Yet as he continued pondering these issues, he came to see the simple truth that God chooses to bless those who seek after him. This revelation relieved him. He recognized that the ability to accept the daily joys of having a good meal and doing one's work could be satisfying if done to the glory of God.

> *That everyone may eat and drink, and find satisfaction*
> *in all his toil—this is the gift of God. (Eccles. 3:13)*

When our work, no matter what kind, is done to glorify God, we will experience a kind of satisfaction that is unknown outside the

Christian life. The apostle Paul brought deeper insight to the joy of committing our work to the Lord.

*Always give yourselves fully to the work
of the Lord, because you know that your labor in
the Lord is not in vain. (1 Cor. 15:58)*

No matter what kind of work we do, if we commit it to God and do it as though he were the direct recipient of our efforts, God will bless us and our labor. But if we approach work hoping it will fill our spiritual void, we will be disappointed. No matter how important or fulfilling our work, it will never meet this need. The same holds true for riches, fame, family, or any thing else the world has to offer. The deep void in our heart can only be filled by a relationship with Jesus Christ.

A PLAN OF ACTION

Finding the right job usually doesn't happen by accident, but planning can often make the successful difference. For example, a landscaper might recognize that his talents and interests lay in designing the landscape and managing jobs rather than working on the installations. With this in mind, he might show his employer some of his designs and ask if he could begin to work in the business office a few days a week. He might eventually learn to consult with clients on design. Depending on the extent of his interest, he could also look into educational opportunities to learn various kinds of design software or even pursue a degree in landscape architecture. Taking some of these steps may mean venturing outside of his comfort zone, but exploring new opportunities and possibilities can bring surprising rewards.

> *God will prove to you how good and acceptable and perfect his will is when he's got his hands on the steering wheel of your life.*
> —STUART AND JILL BRISCOE

PURSUE YOUR INTERESTS AND GIFTS

The most satisfied and productive workers are those who are doing what they enjoy and do best. Romans 12:6 tells us that God has given each of us the ability to do certain things well: "We have different gifts, according to the grace given us."

Why, then, do we often find ourselves in jobs that have little to do with our strengths and interests?

Several things can sway us into accepting an inappropriate job: salary and benefits, the possibility of another upcoming opportunity, or maybe simple timing—we needed a job—they had an opening. Naturally, these issues have to be considered. But we must make a determination to dignify and honor our God-given skills, gifts, and inclinations by letting them become part of our job-search criteria.

When we left the story of Bill, the pressures and frustrations of his new job had landed him in his supervisor's office. In all his years with the company, this was the first time he had received a reprimand.

Bill's boss was concerned. "This isn't like you, Bill. Are you over your head with this new position?"

After some discussion, his boss suggested that he take advantage of the counseling service offered through the employee assistance program. During the counseling process, Bill was able to admit that he felt unprepared for the intense interactions with people that came with the training responsibilities of his new position. However, he was tired of sales and didn't want to return to it.

Bill's counselor told him about the company's retraining program, which was designed to assess an employee's interests and skills and, if possible, place him or her in appropriate positions within the company.

Over the next week, Bill filled out several surveys and questionnaires designed to reveal areas of his interests and strengths. He wasn't surprised to learn that he was best suited for a position that required less contact with people and more time organizing and analyzing information.

After several discussions with his supervisor, a transfer was arranged from the sales department to the company's claims department. Initially he took a reduction in pay and some specialized computer training, but there was a promising future. Best of all Bill loved his new job. For the first time in years the alarm clock didn't signal the beginning of another dreaded day at work.

Sometimes we can't see the solution to our dissatisfaction because we are too close to it. At those times it's wise to seek help from a qualified career counselor or take the initiative to do research on our own.

If you are in a job that isn't right for you, prayerfully take the matter to the Lord. While still in your current job, see a career counselor if you need help determining your strengths and direction. Do your homework before you make a move. The conventional wisdom still prevails—the best time to find a job is when you already have one. The time and energy spent praying, planning, and writing down your employment goals will greatly increase the likelihood for success.

> *Decisions which are made in the light of God's Word are stable and show wisdom.*
> —VONETTE Z. BRIGHT

RELATIONSHIPS ON THE JOB

Finding the right position is only one piece of the puzzle that leads to job satisfaction. Have you ever heard someone say, "I'd like my work if it weren't for the people I work with"? One of the greatest challenges in the workplace is getting along with other people. It hardly matters if someone is the best and the brightest at what he does if he creates dissension in the office. Regardless of whether we're hired to lead or be led, it is the ability to establish functional and healthy workplace relationships that can make or break our success and job satisfaction.

Supervisors have a particular responsibility to create a satisfying and productive atmosphere that encourages others to reach their full potential. To inspire confidence and loyalty from others, a supervisor must lead by example. If he values punctuality, he should be punctual. If he insists on respectful behavior, he should demonstrate it in his treatment of others. If he wants to create a spirit of teamwork, he should do his best to keep workers informed of developments that could affect their department. In other words, a supervisor should practice the Golden Rule in order to create an environment where he himself would want to work.

Relationships among peers can be some of the most competitive and challenging in the workplace. Balance and discretion should be exercised in these associations. Some individuals feel that the only important relationships are with their supervisors. This attitude overlooks both the importance of teamwork and the obvious benefit of building friendships, which in some cases last a lifetime. Peers can constitute a valuable network of shared information and generate an atmosphere of cooperation. When we build goodwill among our coworkers, we contribute to our own feelings of well-being on the job and the well-being of our coworkers as well.

Peers often work in close proximity, so respecting the privacy of others is essential to good working relationships. The primary offender of this unwritten rule is the gossip. It has been said that gossips make mountains out of molehills by adding more dirt. Nothing more thoroughly undermines productivity and morale. "A gossip betrays a confidence; so avoid a man who talks too much" (Prov. 20:19). Good advice. No one is safe from a chronic gossip, and nothing reveals a person's character more completely than what he or she says.

> *Doing an injury puts you below your enemy; revenging an injury makes you even with him; forgiving an injury sets you above him!*
> —UNKNOWN

When virtually every personality type is thrown together to accomplish a common goal, conflicts are inevitable. But when we are mindful of our own behavior and determined to give an honest day's work for our pay, we have already greatly minimized our chances for conflict. It's hard to find fault with this kind of work ethic. If conflicts do arise, they should be handled carefully and prayerfully. Dealing with a conflict quickly at its source is usually the wisest approach. If handled one-on-one it's far less disruptive to the workplace. Confronting interpersonal problems without becoming defensive can really put us to the test. It helps to remember that people generally defend their weaknesses, not their strengths.

INTEGRITY ON THE JOB

Maintaining our Christian integrity on the job can be one of our greatest challenges. It is tempting to compromise our values and ethics at work for the apparent sake of not rocking the boat. Being true to our beliefs and values is not always easy, but it is a solid and wise decision.

This principle was played out dramatically in the life of Daniel. Daniel had been taken captive during the fall of Jerusalem and brought to Babylon. The fact that he was exceptionally intelligent and good-looking distinguished him from the masses, and he, along with three other young Hebrew men, was brought to King Nebuchadnezzar for the purpose of being trained for service in the palace.

This period of training lasted three years. The young men were taught the language and the literature of Babylon. The goal of this prolonged and intensive training was to methodically establish a thoroughly Babylonian mind-set in the trainees. Toward that end, they were also given food from the king's table that consisted of wine and various meats.

> Hold yourself
> responsible to a
> higher standard
> than anyone else
> expects of you.
> Never excuse yourself.
> —HENRY WARD
> BEECHER

Being Jewish, Daniel and his friends were aware that the king's diet would violate the food restrictions set forth in the Mosaic Law. This was a sticky situation. To reject the king's food could be viewed as an insult, yet to accept it violated their beliefs. Daniel, however, did not struggle with his decision:

But Daniel purposed in his heart that he would not defile himself with the portion of the king's delicacies, nor with the wine which he drank; therefore he requested of the chief of the eunuchs that he might not defile himself. (Dan. 1:8 NKJV)

Daniel *purposed in his heart.* This is where Christian integrity begins; we make a decision that our conduct will reflect the beliefs we hold deep in our hearts.

God had already begun working on the guard in charge of Daniel, so when Daniel asked for a simple diet of vegetables and water, the guard was willing to consider his request. The guard's concerns were mostly for himself. If Daniel and his friends looked scrawny and pale, he would be held accountable. To offset his concerns, Daniel proposed that they be allowed to eat their chosen diet for ten days. After that time, they could be judged in comparison to the other young men. At the end of the ten days, Daniel and his friends "looked healthier and better nourished than any of the young men who ate the royal food" (Dan. 1:15). God further rewarded their faithfulness by giving them special knowledge and understanding.

In every matter of wisdom and understanding
about which the king questioned them, he found
them ten times better than all the magicians and
enchanters in his whole kingdom. (Dan. 1:20)

Daniel wasn't militant or "in your face" with his beliefs. His request was humble and depended heavily on God's divine assistance.

Why should we doubt that God is equally anxious to reward our integrity at work? We fear that we may suffer because of our beliefs—and we may. But behaving at odds with our deep beliefs brings enormous stress and inner conflict. A duplicitous life means more than the loss of job satisfaction; it means that we have deprived ourselves of the joys of being true to ourselves and faithful to God.

THE BEAUTY OF BALANCE

Americans are notorious for working too much. We put in too many hours at the office while other important areas of our lives languish due to inattention. Sometimes it's even hard for us to admit that our overwork is a problem. After all, aren't we doing it for the sake of the family? If you suspect that your work life is out of balance, ask yourself how much time you've spent with your family or friends this week, then compare that with the amount of time you've spent at work. The results can be sobering.

Work is undeniably important, but it's only one facet of a well-rounded life. When our job chronically dominates our life, something will eventually give way, such as our walk with the Lord, our health, our marriage, or our friendships. That's why a balanced life also means giving ourselves permission to rest and relax. God created the heavens and the earth in six days, and on the seventh day he rested. God didn't rest because he was tired; rather, he stopped and enjoyed the results of his work. This was a pattern for us to follow so that we might maintain a healthy perspective that enables us to function according to the way we were designed.

A well-ordered life comes from honoring the priorities that are established in God's Word. The Bible tells us that our primary relationship should be with God, followed by the relationship with our spouse. Children, friends, and work follow. Someone wisely said, "No one on their deathbed ever said, 'I wish I'd spent more time at the office.'" Keeping our work within the hierarchy of godly priorities will bring untold blessings and bear witness to the balance of the Christian life.

THE EDGE

Linda glanced at her watch—12:20 P.M.—forty minutes until she was due back from lunch to the law firm where she worked as the receptionist. She had eaten her yogurt at her desk so she would have time to go to the bank and pick up a prescription at the drugstore. No problem—if she didn't linger.

Her high heels tapped a purposeful pace on the busy downtown sidewalk. Dressy clothes were just one of the many changes that had come with working in a professional office after years of waitressing. At first she had been intimidated by the firm's formal atmosphere, but she was beginning to feel more comfortable and enjoy being around the bright, challenging minds. Most importantly, the steady income and benefits were a godsend for herself and her family. Regardless of those times when she felt like a square peg in a round hole, she was determined to do whatever she had to do in order to fit in and keep her job.

Flashing lights from two fire trucks greeted her as she rounded the corner near the bank. A knot of people visored their eyes with their hands and stared at the roof of a five-story parking garage where a slender young man with hands shoved deep into the pockets of his jacket paced nervously and studied the street below.

Oh, no! He's going to jump! Linda thought.

Firemen moved in swift precision both on the street and the rooftop, but when two men cautiously approached him, the young man backed away and moved even closer to the edge. Linda gasped and turned away. She couldn't bear the thought of witnessing such a tragedy. She hurried through the crowd, eyes downcast.

At the drugstore and the bank, she mechanically carried out her business, but her thoughts never left the desperate young man on the roof. Maybe by now the firemen had been able to coax him away from the edge. But as the parking garage came into view, her heart sank to find the man still there, anxiously shifting his weight from one foot to the other.

What could be happening in his life that made death appear to be the only solution? Had he lost his job—his health? Was he estranged from his family? In trouble with the law? Oh, how lonely he looked perched precariously on the edge of the roof—like a bird clinging to a limb in the midst of a storm.

The image brought a Bible verse to Linda's mind and prompted her to pray: "God, you know even when a tiny sparrow falls to the ground, so you must also know this man and his troubles. Don't let go of him. Somehow let him know that you're with him and you care."

As she passed through the gawking crowd, Linda heard someone utter a wisecrack that was followed by an eruption of nervous laughter. She cringed, wondering if the desperate man on the roof could hear. What if the laughter confirmed his feelings of worthlessness? He might even think that the faceless crowd was hoping he would jump.

A thought seemed to come from nowhere: *Get down on your knees and pray for him.*

Linda immediately began praying, but she stopped short of getting on her knees in the midst of this crowd.

The thought persisted: *Get on your knees. Pray!*

Her mind reeled off objections: These people would probably think she was crazy—a religious fanatic. What if someone from her office saw her? Religion was a subject that was never discussed. She looked down at the sidewalk. Would the rough cement snag her stockings or scuff her new high heels?

The thoughts seemed to echo in her ears. Here was a man so desperate that he was considering throwing away the precious gift of his life, and her prideful concerns were preventing her from following the clear urging to kneel in prayer for him!

She set her purse and packages on the sidewalk, lowered herself to her knees, bowed her head, and prayed.

Back in the office Linda joined the group at the conference room window. A cheer went up as an officer inched close to the man and pulled him away from the edge.

Throughout the day the young man was the subject of much conversation. No one ever mentioned seeing Linda kneel in prayer, but she knew it wouldn't have mattered if they had.

She felt an odd connection with the stranger on the roof. Somehow the world had overwhelmed him, and he found himself on the brink of losing everything. In her own way she had been on dangerous ground too. In her desire to keep her job and fit in, she had been on the verge of not being true to her deepest beliefs.

Even now she sometimes thinks of the young man. She prays that he has found hope, and she thanks God for his loving hand that pulled them both back from the edge.

THE SHADOW OF HIS WINGS

Marcia stomped down the hall with the letter Janice had just typed clinched in her fist. Janice looked up from the switchboard and tried to keep her voice from shaking as she answered an incoming call. "Good morning, Western Office Supply."

Marcia loomed over her desk, her mouth set in a hard, straight line. When the call was connected, Marcia threw the letter on her desk.

"Your work is unacceptable! This is the third time I've had to bring this back to have typos corrected!"

Out of the corner of her eye, Janice noticed several coworkers eavesdropping while pretending to study a new fax machine. Color rose to her face.

Marcia continued. "Obviously your head's not in your work. Maybe your problem is that you don't really need a job!"

"I'm sorry," Janice said. "I'll get it corrected and back to you right away."

"That's what you said last time—and the time before that. I don't know what's wrong with you."

Janice was trembling as she answered the next call. In truth she didn't know what was wrong with her either. When she took this job as a switchboard operator and typist, she honestly felt that she could do the work with ease. Her typing had always been accurate and fast—65 words per minute. Now she was making such silly mistakes. And sometimes it seemed that her fingers just wouldn't do what her brain told them to do. Even more perplexing, recently she had noticed that her left arm sometimes fell oddly across her chest rather than loosely at her side. Her sister had urged her to see a doctor, and now it seemed that she must if she wanted to keep her job.

At noon she took her lunch to the picnic table in the courtyard. She was getting accustomed to eating alone. Since Marcia began her relentless criticism, Janice's friends at work were suddenly too busy to have lunch with her. For weeks it seemed that Marcia was watching for any opportunity to attack and humiliate her.

She opened her Bible and read Psalm 57. In it David cried out to God to save him from those who were tormenting him—"I will take refuge in the shadow of your wings until the disaster has passed" (Ps. 57:1). Janice longed to feel God's protection, but she felt so terribly alone. All she could do was read the Word and pray.

The next week in the doctor's office she learned that all the initial medical tests were normal. Her sister, however, wasn't satisfied. She insisted that they continue looking for answers, so they made an appointment with a neurologist. After only a few minutes in his office, he reached a tentative diagnosis: Parkinson's disease. The disease causes muscle rigidity due to the absence of a vital chemical in the brain that enables messages to travel to the nerve endings.

With the diagnosis, fear mingled with an odd sense of relief. At least there was a reason for what was happening to her. Immediately she arranged to meet with Marcia and Rob, the department head.

On the day of the meeting, Marcia wore a steely expression and carried a folder that doubtless contained evidence of Janice's poor performance. Janice, however, took the lead in the meeting and was matter-of-fact in discussing her diagnosis. "This is why I've had problems with typing. I hope the medication will help, but I'll need your patience as I learn to cope with this." Rob was openly sympathetic, but Marcia's expression never changed as she silently stared at the floor.

One change, however, was immediate; the harassment about her work performance stopped. Marcia wasn't warm with her, but she was civil and patient when waiting for corrections. Sometimes as she stood by the desk, Janice sensed that she wanted to say something, but she never did.

Several weeks later Janice had stayed late to clean up the kitchen when Marcia walked in. They exchanged *hellos* and Janice turned to leave.

"No. Wait," said Marcia. "Just a minute—please."

Janice stopped. Marcia had never before said *please* to her.

"You know, I've never told you how sorry I am about your illness. I hope you understand that I never would have been so hard on you if I'd known."

Janice nodded. "I understand," she said quietly.

"Really?" Marcia fidgeted with the tassels on her belt. "You know, I don't really understand you. All those times I yelled at you, you never once yelled back. Even after you found out you were sick, you didn't retaliate or try to turn people against me for being so mean to you." Marcia gave a short laugh. "I'm not sure I could have passed up such an opportunity! I'd see you by yourself at lunch reading your Bible. I couldn't get over how strong and dignified you were even when I knew I was making it tough on you."

Janice was tempted to tell her about the pain she'd felt during that time—how her self-esteem had been trampled, how embarrassed and hurt she'd been. But she didn't. Somehow, it seemed irrelevant.

Then Marcia said what Janice had never even imagined hearing. "I'm sorry, Janice. I hope you can forgive me."

After their conversation she wondered if her supervisor would really change. Marcia did seem to soften a bit, and as a result, the atmosphere of the entire office was more relaxed. Janice feels that the biggest change has been in herself. Looking back, she can see that even during the most difficult times, God was sheltering her under his wing. When she had felt her most vulnerable, Marcia had seen God's strength in her.

Janice is confronting a new adversary now: Parkinson's disease. She does her best to fight the good fight, and she remembers that even when she doesn't feel his presence, God is there, and he will never abandon her.

Labor of Love

Doug brushed the dust from his shirt and adjusted his tool belt as he stepped onto the elevator in the professional building where he was doing electrical work on a tenant build-out. As the doors were closing, a group of lawyers stepped onto the elevator. They carried boxy briefcases and talked in low voices about trial preparations.

Although they were standing directly across from Doug, none of them made eye contact or acknowledged him in any way. It was unspoken, but obvious: they were professionals, what did they have in common with a dusty, common laborer?

We have more in common than you think! thought Doug.

In 1973, Doug had been in college. He was impressed with Sam Ervin, the senator from North Carolina who was the chairman of the committee that investigated the Watergate incident and the 1972 election campaign. Ervin was an old-fashioned country lawyer, who carried a copy of the Constitution in his pocket and quoted from it liberally. He brought his common sense, deep knowledge, and high standards to Washington during a time when those qualities were desperately needed. Doug had been considering a career in law, and Sam Ervin's example during that dark period in our country was just the inspiration he needed to go on to law school.

Also while he was in college, another man had a profound influence on his life: Billy Graham. Doug watched a crusade on television one evening, and in the quiet of his room, he made the decision to receive Christ as his Savior. He began reading the Bible, going to church, and growing steadily in his faith.

Law school proved to be a consuming endeavor. He was working part time and studying constantly when he wasn't in class. But he graduated, passed the bar exam, and joined the throng of other fresh graduates looking for positions in law firms.

He ended up in the DA's office prosecuting low-level crimes such as shoplifting, bad checks, and DWIs. It was a grind, with one case following another in an endless stream. The office was understaffed and underpaid. Doug learned that wealthy people who could afford to hire big-name lawyers received a different justice than the poor.

Over the three years he spent there, his idealism took a beating. But it was also during this time that he met Lynn. She was spontaneous and funny—a breath of fresh air into a stale existence. They fell in love and were married.

After three years in the DA's office, Doug decided to strike out on his own. He opened a small office, and Lynn worked as his secretary. Maybe he could begin to fulfill that dream of being an old-fashioned country lawyer. Now that he had the control, he would set standards for his office. He would not do divorces or criminal cases.

He learned right away that keeping the doors open to his small office open meant taking almost every case that came his way. Soon he was in another kind of grind; he felt like he was running a wills-and-estates mill.

The more he learned about being a lawyer, the more disillusioned he became. Many attorneys were up-front and ethical, but others had no qualms about canceling hearings, stringing out depositions that should have only taken an hour into hours-long ordeals. These were often calculated inefficiencies, and in the end it was the clients that were hurt.

Doug decided that maybe he would be better suited as a judge. He ran for municipal judge in a small, newly incorporated city. He won. For nine years he sat on the bench and generally enjoyed his work. He also enjoyed the respect and prestige. It was nice to be seated at the head table at various dinners and functions. He grew accustomed to being called "Your Honor" and having his word held in high regard.

During this time some needed changes to his position were presented to the judicial reform committee. Unfortunately, during the process, these sensible petitions were obscured by political motives. His recommendations were voted down. Doug felt had no avenue for recourse, so he resigned.

He was confident that he could find a position in a law firm, but after a year of searching without success, he grew discouraged and depressed. Fortunately, Lynn had a good job at a law firm, and they were getting by.

Through their church Lynn had learned about an organization called Laborers for Christ. Individuals in this group went around the country building churches, educational complexes, church additions, or whatever construction project the church needed. She mentioned it to Doug.

"It only pays minimum wage, and you have to get yourself there and provide your own accommodations for the duration of the project," she said, "but it might be refreshing and interesting."

It couldn't have been further from Doug's experience or the kind of work he had been looking for, but it sounded like it might be an adventure. They prayed about it.

On a Friday afternoon, Doug submitted his application, and on Monday he was accepted and told to report to the job site on Long Island as soon as possible. After a solid year of one having door after another slamming in his face, he felt that this must be where the Lord had been leading him. He kissed Lynn good-bye and set off across the country in a beat-up pickup truck with a pop-up camper that would be his home for the next six months.

The first day on the job was an eye-opener, to say the least. The day began in a way that would become routine—a group devotional of singing, a brief Bible study, and prayer. Doug was sure of one thing—he would need the prayer!

Their project was to build an educational complex to adjoin the existing church building. He didn't have a clue about what he was supposed to do. The foreman patiently showed him a few things and put him to work. The other four were all retired from construction-related careers. Although they were twenty to thirty years older than Doug, they were working circles around him.

That night he fairly crawled into his tiny 8' by 10' home and collapsed into bed. Muscles hurt that he didn't even know he had. Before he plummeted into sleep, he prayed, "Oh, God, what have I gotten myself into?"

Over the next few weeks, he fell into a routine. The men were patient with him, and he was learning quickly. Generally, he had to be told only once how to do something. At the end of the day, he was still exhausted, but the foreign feeling of physical labor was giving way to a new satisfaction. He knew he had done something during that day that would benefit people for years to come. It felt great!

Now, he had another challenge facing him. Each man was to take a turn leading the Bible teaching portion of the morning devotional.

"Have you decided what you're going to talk about," asked Lynn on the phone one evening.

"Not yet," he said. "You know, when I was a lawyer, I used to talk to the judge or jury with the goal of trying to impress them to think a certain way, but that's not what this is about. It has to come from my heart, not my head."

The next few days were spent framing the roof. He had never been comfortable with heights, and here he was standing on a ladder swinging a hammer. He couldn't imagine doing this for anyone but the Lord!

As he worked, he thought of the story in the Bible about the men who brought their paralyzed friend to see Jesus. The crowd surrounding Jesus was so thick that they couldn't even get close to him, so they hoisted their friend's pallet to the top of the house, made a hole in the roof, and lowered him before Jesus. When Jesus saw their faith, he healed the man. As Doug hammered on the church roof, he thought, *I wonder who fixed the hole in the roof?* The Lord had just given him his teaching for the devotional he was to lead the next morning!

For the next three and a half years, Doug was assigned to one project after another. He worked in Los Angeles, Chicago, New Mexico, and New Hampshire building everything from a children's theater to a church from the ground up.

It was time to return to his home and Lynn. However, when he left Laborers for Christ, there were no thoughts of returning to law. Instead, his winding career path now led him to become an electrician—an occupation that continues to bring him hard work and satisfaction.

When he was a lawyer, he had become bogged down in his own interests and goals. As a result, he lost his perspective on God, himself, and even his fellowman. The Lord had to shake him up, humble him a bit, and give him a fresh perspective—from the rooftop of a church.

LOOKING BACK ON LESSONS LEARNED

- If we approach our work with thoughtful care and attention, the result will be greater productivity, competence, and satisfaction.
- Work can seem like a necessary evil unless we are doing what we enjoy and feel called to do by God.
- Finding the work that is right for us requires conscious planning, patient preparation, and prayer.
- Our work does not define who we are, but who we are usually defines the quality of our work.
- Knowing how to get along with others is essential to surviving and thriving in the workplace.
- Having the courage to confront work problems early on can diffuse or eliminate conflict and unpleasantness down the road.
- If we want our lives to honor God, we must be committed to maintaining our values and integrity in the workplace. Nothing exceeds the power and influence of a good example. This is our daily witness.
- When we are slow to criticize and quick to listen, we will win the respect and trust of others.
- We will reap what we sow, whether evil or good.
- At the end of our life, work accomplishments will pale in comparison to our loving relationships with family and friends.
- Work can be a great source of satisfaction, but it can't satisfy the deepest need of our soul. Only a personal relationship with Jesus Christ can do that.

8

Tending Your Treasure:
Seeking Financial Perspective

*"For where your treasure is,
there your heart will be also."*
MATTHEW 6:21

Of all the rotten luck, thought Jane. Her husband, John, had flipped to a TV station airing a program about debt. The discussion centered on credit card debt and the financial quicksand of carrying big balances at high interest rates. The host of the show stressed the point that the first step to regaining financial stability is to confront the situation and then make a plan for eliminating the high-interest debt.

When the program broke for commercial, John turned to Jane and asked the question she had been dreading for months: "Just how far in debt are we, anyway?"

Jane kept the books and managed the finances for their family plumbing business. She was also in charge of the personal finances for their family of thirteen children. It was an arrangement that seemed to make sense and enabled Jane to stay at home with the children while helping with the business.

The problem with credit sprang from another problem. A few years back Jane and John took out a home improvement loan to do some major renovations that would accommodate the needs of their large and growing family. The house had been in their family for four generations and desperately needed to be updated and enlarged. Early on, it was easy to see that the project was exceeding their budget. The home improvement loan was soon exhausted, but the expenses continued. That was when Jane first slipped the credit card across the counter. She justified her actions by telling herself that they had to finish the house, and she would pay off the balance quickly by "zapping it down" with large payments.

But more and more frequently she presented one of their many credit cards when she was at the checkout counter. Not only was she charging expenses related to the renovation; she was now charging toys and clothes for the children. She even found herself buying things she knew they could do without. It was so easy—just present the credit card and walk out with the goods.

> The best way
> to get on your
> feet is to get
> on your knees.
> —UNKNOWN

On those occasions when John asked how they were doing financially, she would shrug and say, "Oh, okay." She tried not to think about the growing debt, and only recently had she gathered the nerve to tally the bottom line on their credit card balances. It was over $50,000! She had intended to tell John, but she hadn't been prepared for it at this moment.

John was stunned and understandably angry at the revelation. "What were you thinking?" he asked. Jane tried to explain how the initial need subtly shifted to a compelling habit. Her excuses sounded ridiculous, even to herself. She sat quietly and waited for John's anger to subside. When the dust finally settled, the two did something they hadn't done in a long time; they sat down together and honestly discussed their finances.

A COMMON PROBLEM

Even if we haven't succumbed to the lure of easy and costly credit, learning to manage our money can be one of the most challenging aspects of our lives. The challenge is a common one as evidenced by the fact that financial problems are among the leading reasons cited for divorce. Believers are not exempt from the usual concerns of bills, debt, earnings, savings, and retirement. However, there should be a fundamental distinction between a worldly attitude and a Christian attitude toward money and possessions. The Bible tells us that *everything* belongs to God (see Ps. 50:10–12), and we are only stewards of what he has graciously entrusted to us. Because stewardship means managing someone else's money or property, it carries the elements of responsibility and accountability. The fact that we are managing God's money and property requires a significant shift in perspective toward money that slightly removes us from the prideful involvement that often comes with ownership.

In the Parable of the Talents (Matt. 25:14–30) we see this concept in action. The master of three servants *gave* them various amounts of money to manage. From the beginning, the men understood that they were not the owners of the money, but the guardians. The master expected them to be wise and resourceful with his money; otherwise he would have left it in the bank to passively earn interest.

Similarly, the Lord wants us to be wise and resourceful with the means he has entrusted to us. Of course we are to provide for the needs of our family, but a believer's view of money and property extends to how they can be used as tools for accomplishing godly goals in the

He who buries his talent is making a grave mistake.
—UNKNOWN

world. Like the good stewards in the parable, we should be motivated to one day hear the Lord say to us, "Well done, good and faithful servant! You have been faithful with a few things; I will put you in charge of many things. Come and share your master's happiness" (Matt. 25:21). If we live and operate in the knowledge that all we have belongs to God, one day we will hear these wonderful words.

THE BIBLE'S VIEW ON MONEY

The problem comes with compartmentalized thinking. We convince ourselves that money, salary, and spending are elements of the nitty-gritty real world, but that church, the Bible, and Christianity are in the softer realm of spirituality. The Bible makes no such distinction. Responsibly handling our money is just another aspect of the Christian walk. In fact, of all the parables Jesus told, almost half concerned money. These parables contain practical and timeless messages about the risk, responsibility, rewards, and the snares of handling our money. Jesus plainly warned us not to allow the love and pursuit of money to dominate our lives:

> *"No one can serve two masters. Either he will*
> *hate the one and love the other, or he will be*

devoted to the one and despise the other.
You cannot serve both God and Money." (Matt. 6:24)

In a day when it's common to hear people shamelessly reveal the most intimate and embarrassing aspects of their relationships, facts about income and spending are still largely off limits. Maybe that's because deep down we know that our spending habits divulge more about our character and beliefs than we care to reveal.

For instance, if your checkbook fell into a stranger's hands, could he look at the register and tell what you treasure the most? Would he find a thoughtful manager with a generous heart or see a pattern of foolish spending and indulgence? Jesus knew that an obsession to obtain and acquire "treasure" revealed the true priorities of our lives.

"Do not store up for yourselves treasures on earth, where
moth and rust destroy, and where thieves break in and steal.
But store up for yourselves treasures in heaven, where moth
and rust do not destroy, and where thieves do not break in
and steal. For where your treasures is,
there your heart will be also." (Matt. 6:19–21)

If we are consumed with the ownership of anything, that thing has become our master.

The perspective on money is never sharper than when viewed from the vantage point of the end of life. In the Parable of the Rich Fool, the prosperous and greedy farmer gleefully made plans to hoard his bountiful crops by tearing down his old barns and building bigger ones.

"But God said to him, 'You fool! This very night your
life will be demanded from you. Then who will get
what you have prepared for yourself?'" (Luke 12:20)

The man pictured a merry future of eating and drinking when, in reality, his life was about to end. Now his riches would be enjoyed by someone else, while he entered eternity without a shred of stored treasured for his eternal future.

The pitfalls of money are not reserved for the rich. Financial worries and pressures can drain our joy and rob us of precious peace of mind. In the Parable of the Sower, Jesus said, "Still others, like seed sown among thorns, hear the word; but the worries of this life, the deceitfulness of wealth and the desires for other things come in and choke the word, making it unfruitful" (Mark 4:18–19). Worldly worries, money problems, preoccupation with business, and ambitions to become rich distract us from spiritual and eternal matters.

When we are consumed with paying off debt and keeping the family clothed and fed, giving often falls to the wayside. As a result, we deprive ourselves of the blessings that come with giving. Paul reminded the Philippians, however, that their abundance was a direct result of their generosity to further the spread of the gospel.

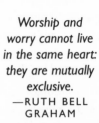

Worship and worry cannot live in the same heart: they are mutually exclusive.
—RUTH BELL GRAHAM

> *And my God will meet all your needs according to*
> *his glorious riches in Christ Jesus. (Phil. 4:19)*

It seems obvious that Satan can use our finances to keep us enslaved and distracted from our relationship with Christ. Yet we are often our own worst enemies when it comes to achieving financial balance. In the story of Jane and the problems brought on by her runaway credit card use, only discipline and denial would remedy the situation.

Jane was determined to get her family out of debt. Yet she realized that she lacked the fundamental knowledge to begin managing the finances wisely. The first thing she did was go to the Christian bookstore and buy two books: *The Financially Confident Woman* by Mary Hunt and *Debt-Free Living* by Larry Burkett. She read them and immediately began to implement their advice.

She and John had several more sessions in which they prayed together, established a budget, and set a regular salary amount for themselves. They cut up the credit cards, and Jane kept record of her progress in paying off the balances.

One of the most difficult challenges along the road of good intentions was Christmas. In the past Christmas had been a time of unguarded spending in order to make a memorable Christmas for their thirteen children. But this time, Jane and John called the kids together and told them honestly that their finances wouldn't allow for abundance under the tree. They were surprised and pleased when the kids were immediately supportive and understanding. Their oldest son came to them later and told them he had everything he needed and didn't need any gifts at all. That Christmas remains one of the dearest and most memorable of their family Christmases.

It's been a long haul, but Jane and John can finally see the light at the end of the tunnel. Their debts are almost paid, and they have new peace and purpose in managing their finances.

STORING UP TREASURES IN HEAVEN

Many companies offer their employees a payroll deduction plan. Before the paycheck ever hits the hand of the employee, a certain amount has been taken out for savings, retirement accounts, medical benefits, and taxes. When the initial commitment is made, the loss is noticeable, and we may even regret having a smaller paycheck.

> What we are
> is more significant,
> in the long run,
> than what we do.
> It is impossible
> for a man to
> give what he
> does not have.
> —ELTON TRUEBLOOD

Eventually, however, we adapt to the new amount, and our savings account begins to grow. A similar discipline can help bring about an investment in a treasure that will not fade away. When Jesus told us to seek his kingdom first, he was telling us how to prioritize our lives.

> But seek first his kingdom and his righteousness, and all
> these things will be given to you as well. Therefore do not
> worry about tomorrow, for tomorrow will worry about itself.
> Each day has enough trouble of its own." (Matt. 6:33–34)

When each day is lived with Christ as our priority, the matters that typically preoccupy our minds and energies fall into a godly order. We understand biblical financial concepts and take the time to prayerfully budget and plan, but we know that this treasure on earth is fleeting and fickle.

A LASTING TREASURE

Treasure is spoken of in the Bible but with quite a different connotation. Paul said that "we have this treasure in jars of clay to show that this all-surpassing power is from God and not from us" (2 Cor. 4:7). He was referring to the lasting treasure of the gospel of Jesus Christ. He described true wealth and treasure to the Colossians in these words:

> My purpose is that they may be encouraged in heart and
> united in love, so that they may have the full riches of
> complete understanding, in order that they may know
> the mystery of God, namely Christ, in whom are hidden
> all the treasures of wisdom and knowledge. (Col. 2:2–3)

The mystery is revealed to us: our true wealth comes from the assurance of a relationship with Jesus. He is our Treasure—a truth that is hidden from unbelievers but should be uppermost in our minds.

> Keep your lives free from the love of money and be
> content with what you have, because God has said, "Never
> will I leave you; never will I forsake you." (Heb. 13:5)

Materialism has the potential to derail our spiritual walk by imitating the fulfillment that can only be found in Christ. With God's help, we can find balance and peace.

On Solid Ground

Eric looked at his watch—lunchtime. He got up from his desk, shrugged on his suit coat, and left the office.

This should be interesting, he thought. Donald, a good friend from college, had invited him to lunch to hear about an "exciting investment opportunity."

Normally, Eric wouldn't have been interested, but lately, Donald seemed to have the Midas touch where investing was concerned. Even though Donald wasn't in the business himself, he had read, studied, and trained himself. Apparently his efforts had paid off. Over the last few years, he had made a small fortune by taking some calculated risks in the stock market.

"This sounds like an incredible, ground-floor investment opportunity," he told Eric when he phoned. "But, I'll tell you up front, it's probably pretty risky. Do you have a little daredevil left in you after all those years of domestic bliss?"

"Not much," Eric admitted, "but it can't hurt to listen."

Because Donald was single and made a good salary, he had something that Eric found hard to understand—disposable income. When an opportunity came up that interested him, he had the necessary resources and only himself to consult.

Eric's situation was quite a different story. He and Jenny managed their money with care and lots of mutual consultation. A few years ago they had made a financial plan, and they had stuck with it. Even though their kids were preschoolers, he and Jenny already had a good start on their college funds. Thanks, mostly, Eric realized, to Jenny's discipline and good judgment.

At lunch, the enthusiasm was palpable. Two of the company's partners explained that the new venture was planning to produce new technology-oriented products for the health-care industry. It sounded impressive, though neither Eric nor Donald had a background that enabled them to totally understand the products or their medical applications.

The partners showed them the business plan and a projection of return on their individual investments. It was incredible. Eric realized that if it even came close to what they anticipated, it could one day mean early retirement for him and Jenny.

Donald was openly enthusiastic, but Eric was characteristically restrained. "I want to run this by my financial advisor and by my wife."

The partners seemed a little let down when they realized that no commitment would be made at lunch, but the meeting ended positively.

"Do what you have to do, but we need a definite yes or no tomorrow. Things are moving quickly. If you're not in, we've got other people who'll jump at it."

Eric nodded. "I understand. I'll get back to you first thing in the morning."

Back at his office he faxed some of the information to Ned, his financial advisor. In a few minutes he got a call from his office telling him that Ned was out of town until the beginning of next week.

Eric was disappointed and concerned. Ned knew Eric and Jenny and their financial situation and goals. He had always been a reliable source of sound advice as well as strong, godly counsel.

Too bad this thing is so rushed, thought Eric. *Well, Jenny and I will just have to do our best to decide on our own.*

Over dinner Eric told Jenny about his lunch meeting. "It's a ground-floor opportunity, and they just don't come along that often." To his surprise she was intrigued.

She poured them each a cup of coffee. "It sounds like it really has potential, and I like the idea that the products will help people. If it goes the way they say, we could be financially secure! How many young couples can say that?" She sipped her coffee. "What bothers me is that we don't really understand the product, and they're in such a rush! I wish we could wait a few days and see what Ned had to say about it."

"I'm concerned about those same things," said Eric.

"You know," said Jenny, "this morning as I was reading, a statement the author made really jumped out at me. He said, 'Satan pushes, but God leads.' I can't help but feel a little pushed, do you?"

"Yeah," said Eric. "But I'm not sure that's enough of a reason not to do it. Why don't we pray about it and then sleep on it. In the morning we'll see how we feel before we make our final decision."

The next morning Eric was lathering shaving lotion on his face when Jenny came in. "How do you feel about things this morning?" she asked.

"I still have mixed feelings," he said. "I wish I didn't—I wish I felt a clear-cut positive or negative. How about you?"

"You know, when we were talking about it at dinner, I was so focused on what that money could mean to us in the long run that it made all my other doubts seem trivial. But last night I just tossed and turned and worried all night. I had one strange dream after another."

Eric toweled his face. "What are your worries?"

"Pretty much the same things we talked about last night. I keep wondering how we can justify investing so much money in something we don't really understand. And then I hate feeling rushed and not having time to get Ned's opinion."

"Same here. Maybe we . . . ."

"Wow!" Jenny interrupted. "Sorry, but I just remembered one of my dreams! We were standing in a building that was under construction when the cement began to crack under our feet! At first we thought it was an earthquake, but it wasn't. We had to run to get out of it."

They were quiet for a little while as they considered this.

"I know it was just a dream," said Eric, "but maybe the Lord's warning us."

"Do you think?"

"We've got a lot of questions. We feel pressured, and it's a lot of money we're considering investing," said Eric. "I think we'd better let this pass."

Jenny nodded her head. "I think you're right. Too bad, though. It just might be a great deal, but we asked God to give us peace if it was, and we sure don't feel peaceful."

Later that morning Eric called Donald from the office. "We passed on the investment, Donald. I've already phone the partners and let them know, but thanks for thinking of us."

Donald understood. "Can I ask why you decided against it?"

Eric hesitated, but then told him about their major concerns. "Jenny and I prayed about it last night. We asked God to give us peace about it if it was the right thing for us to do. Then Jenny tossed and turned all night. We just didn't feel like it was the right thing for us to do."

"You know, that's interesting," said Donald, "because I haven't felt good about it either. I might have gone ahead, but hearing about yours and Jenny's reservations—I'm going to pass, too." Then he added, "It must be nice to have a wife to discuss this kind of thing with. "

"It is," said Eric. "Sometimes we come at things from different points of view, and it can be frustrating, but I've learned that Jenny's often more sensitive to God's leading than I am. She's usually tuned in when it comes to finding God's will."

About six months later Eric got a call from Donald. "Did you hear?" he asked.

"About what?"

"I just read in the newspaper that the company we were going to invest in went belly-up and left all the investors high and dry! Just think of all the money we would have lost. If you had listened to all my hype about getting in on the ground floor, you and Jenny would have lost all your money. Man, I would have felt terrible!"

"Well, it sounded awfully good to us at first, too—too good, as it turns out, " said Eric. "Maybe getting in on the ground floor is only a good opportunity if you're sure you're building on solid ground."

FIRST FRUITS

Roger sat at his desk hunched over a stack of bills. The calculator hummed as he punched in a stream of numbers. Mary watched him take off his glasses and pinch the bridge of his nose. He looked burdened with worry.

She came up behind him and rubbed his neck and shoulders. "How's it going?" she asked.

"Mary, I don't understand it, but we're not making any real progress. Every time it looks like we might get a little ahead, something comes up, and we're behind the eight ball again."

Even though Roger made a decent salary, they perpetually struggled with money. A few years ago they realized that their spending and their use of credit cards were out of control, so they disciplined themselves, cut up the cards, and learned to curb their spending. Yet after all this time, their balances still were not paid off. In another effort to conserve, they decided to keep their car instead of trading up as they usually did every couple of years. Despite these and other money-saving measures, every month they found themselves out of money days before their next paycheck.

"I think we're making good financial decisions now, yet our savings account is a joke. And in only a few years we'll have college expenses starting for the kids."

Mary had been dreading talking to Roger about a much smaller but pressing financial matter. "I hate to bring this up now, but do you remember the Bible study group I've been organizing for the neighborhood kids?"

Roger nodded.

"Well, it starts in a few weeks, and I still need to buy Bibles and other materials for it."

"How much do you think you'll need?" he asked.

"I priced everything. It will be about sixty dollars," Mary said.

Roger looked at their checkbook and shook his head. "It doesn't look like we're going to have a penny extra this month. Could you ask the kids' parents to pay for the materials?"

"I thought about that, but some of these kids come from homes where the idea of reading the Bible has never even crossed their minds. Asking the parents to come up with money might give them a reason not to let their child come. I think it's important that the materials are furnished."

"I know this is a priority, Mary, and we'll try to take care of it. But, honestly, unless some money falls out of the sky—well, we'll have to wait and see. It sure makes me realize how much I want to be able to do this kind of thing as well as to support our own church's missions." He sighed. "Maybe someday."

He seemed so sad and defeated that Mary let the matter drop. But in church the next day, the subject came up again in a message that focused on the practice of biblical giving.

Although they were familiar principles, it was as though Roger and Mary were hearing the information in a totally fresh way. The pastor emphasized the importance of giving God the "firstfruits" of our labor. He said that in ancient times, the first ripe fruits on the tree were picked and given to support the priesthood. Inherent in those fruits was the promise of the entire harvest to come. The act of giving the first and the best indicated their faith and conviction that God held their future in his hands.

"We often approach our giving in exactly the opposite way," the pastor said. "We wait to see if there are any leftovers in the bank account that we can scrape together to give to God. We hand him the pennies and pocket lint and call it done. I challenge you to honor God by giving him the cream of your earnings—the best that you have. Pluck your firstfruits and present them to him, and enjoy the blessings it brings."

In the car on the way home from church, Roger took Mary's hand and squeezed it. "Mary, I think we've had good intentions but wrong priorities. From now on, starting with our very next paycheck, we're going to make giving to the Lord's work our first priority. Whether it makes sense on paper or not, let's just do it and trust the rest to him."

Roger was true to his word. In addition to the church's missions, he gave Mary ten dollars toward the supplies she needed. It was obvious that he was feeling more peaceful and hopeful than he had in years. The agony of stretching their paycheck had been transformed into the far simpler matter of discipline and obedience.

As the first day of the Bible study grew near, Mary continued to pray for the kids and her needs. "Father, you know I would love to have the fun materials for the kids, but with or without them, we will have a Bible study. Thank you, Father."

About a week later, Mary walked back from the mailbox while sorting through the mail. The familiar handwriting of her best friend, Carol, seemed to shine through the circulars and bills. She eagerly opened the envelope and smiled as she held up a check—for fifty dollars!

"I've been thinking of you so much lately," the card read. "I felt prompted to send this to you—hope it comes at a good time. In Christ's Love, Carol"

The perfect time! Mary smiled.

Since then God has continued to honor their faithfulness. They rarely have a great excess of money, but in addition to meeting their daily needs, their credit card debt is finally paid in full, and a college fund is steadily growing—pretty incredible fruits of their decision to be obedient in their giving. As sweet as the financial peace has been, nothing has exceeded the simple joy of being in line with God's plan. They love giving their best to the Savior who gave his all for them. That's the sweetest fruit of all.

UNMORTGAGED HEARTS

Even as a grown woman Marilyn clearly remembers hearing her father on the phone with his creditors. His spiel was pretty much the same, whether it was the gas company, the mortgage company, or the credit card company.

"We've had a temporary dip in our cash flow," he would say, "but I'll have something for you in a couple of weeks."

His normally strong voice sounded strained—a thin veneer of confidence brushed over his ever-present worry.

After he hung up the phone, her mother would challenge him. "Just how are you going to manage that? You've already promised your entire paycheck to other creditors!"

He would glare at her angrily. "I had to buy some time. What do you want me to do, say 'I haven't got any money now or in the fore-seeable future; why don't you just come pick up the car?'"

And then they would be off and running—arguing over the constant stresses, worries, and problems for which Marilyn could easily see they were equally responsible. She would quietly leave the room and retreat to the safety and peace of her bedroom. *Why don't they just sell this huge house, big cars, and all their stuff so we can be a happy, loving family?*

The only thing she ever heard them fight about was money. They were good people, who probably would have had a good marriage, but they couldn't or wouldn't control their spending even when the consequences dominated their lives.

Her father may have actually believed he would pay off his bills, but he and her mother continued buying things, guaranteeing they would never reduce their mountain of debt. Their solution was for her mother to go to work full time as a secretary. Therefore, when she was only nine, Marilyn started coming home from school to spend empty hours in an empty house. In their concern for her safety, she was not allowed to have friends over, nor could she go to their houses. Day after day she sat in the den by herself and watched television until her parents came home.

Even with these measures, their debt was eventually so deep and delinquent that they filed for bankruptcy. The relief it brought was brief, but the consequences were a constant source of embarrassment, limitations, and anger between them.

Marilyn wanted a different life for herself and her own family. When she met her future husband, Bob, she told him right away that she wanted to live a simple life that wasn't ruled by money and possessions.

"When the time comes for us to start our family," she said, "I want to be able to stay at home. I don't want to drop them at a baby-sitter's house so that she can raise my children, while I go work to pay for an expensive house or cars. What sense does that make? And I've seen up-close what money worries can do to a marriage and family. I don't ever want to risk that."

She didn't have to convince Bob. He shared her views completely.

When they married, they moved into an inexpensive but tiny apartment. Soon they realized that they needed a bigger place. They were both working during those early years, and they considered buying a small home. But when they talked it through, they realized it would take both of their paychecks to qualify for a loan and manage the mortgage payments. They decided not to do anything until they had prayed for guidance.

Within a few days a friend of Bob's offered to sell them a mobile home for no money down and payments that were actually lower than they were currently paying for their apartment. They leaped at the opportunity.

During this time all their friends seemed to be buying homes and starting their families. Marilyn and Bob were constantly buying housewarming gifts and admiring their friends' new homes. They decided they would meet with a realtor just to discuss buying a home. The realtor assured them that with their combined incomes, they could qualify for a nice house. But when Bob and Marilyn said they wanted to qualify on Bob's salary alone, the choices dwindled. They were disappointed, but they decided to stay put.

A few years later, they had a more pressing consideration. They wanted to start their family, which meant they definitely needed to move. The low payments on the mobile home had enabled them to save some money, and they felt sure they could sell the mobile home for a modest profit. When the time came, they knew they would have enough money for a decent down payment.

Again they were told that they could afford a nice home on both of their incomes. The realtor even sat down with them and showed them how, with normal increases to Bob's salary, he would eventually be able to cover the entire mortgage payment out of his salary alone. It was tempting. They both liked the house and by now were very eager to start their family.

When they left the realtor's office, Marilyn asked, "Well, what do you think?"

Bob was quiet for a long moment. "I think if we're not careful, we could easily find ourselves backed into a stressed-out situation over money. And that's just what we don't want. If you're going to quit your job and stay home once we have kids, we have to be sure we're making the decisions now that will make that possible. Let's wait and trust God to help us find something we know for sure we can afford."

It was hard to readjust their thinking and let go of the idea of owning that house. But several months later they learned of a small three-bedroom ranch-style home. It was in a good neighborhood and had a nice, fenced yard—just perfect for kids. They made an offer and applied for a low-interest VA loan on Bob's salary alone. They got the loan, the house, and a mortgage payment that Bob could handle out of his single salary.

They feel that those early decisions and the hard task of delaying what they so badly wanted at the moment really paid off in the long run. It would have been easy to succumb to the lure of a home that was too expensive and to find themselves caught in the trap of working their hearts out for a mortgage. But God honored their commitment to make their family the true priority in their lives. They have never regretted waiting for a house they could afford and saving their hearts for much better things.

Looking Back on Lessons Learned

- If we are consumed with the ownership of anything, that thing has momentarily become our master. We can either be the masters of our money and possessions, or they will master us.
- Worldly worries, money problems, preoccupation with business, and ambitions to become rich distract us from spiritual and eternal matters and rob us of our peace of mind.
- Satan loves it when we're preoccupied with thoughts of money because we are no longer occupied with thoughts of God.
- The first step toward financial stability is to squarely face our money problems.
- Husbands and wives have the great privilege and power of praying together about their finances.

- If we are not giving generously to God's work and others in need, it may signal the need to make spiritual changes.
- When we limit our giving, we limit what God can do in our lives: "Give and it will be given to you" (Luke 6:38).
- Conquering debt often involves the disciplines of cutting up credit cards, curbing impulsive spending, denying our wants, and determining to reach the goal of being debt-free.
- Gratitude is the antidote to greed. If we find ourselves complaining about what we don't have, it's a sure sign that we are not thanking God for what we do have.
- We should beware of being pushed into hasty decisions. It's been said that Satan pushes, but God leads.
- Long-term financial commitments need to harmonize with long-term family goals. If they contradict one another, we must stop and reevaluate before making a commitment.
- Everything we have belongs to God, and we must be wise and faithful stewards of what he has entrusted to us.
- When we seek God's kingdom as our first priority, other matters fall into appropriate order and scale. A believer's true and enduring treasure is Jesus Christ.

9
—

Been There, Didn't Do That:
Dealing with Regrets

For of all the sad words of tongue or pen,
The saddest are these: "It might have been!"
JOHN GREENLEAF WHITTIER

*F*rank Sinatra made big money with his song "My Way." In it he
admits to "a few" regrets, but as he looks back on his life, he has
an overall feeling of pride that comes from knowing that he did life
his way.

Anyone who has had serious regrets in life will tell you that such
an admission would feel more like a judgment than a comfort. The
last thing we experience when we are under the shadow of regret is
bravado and pride.

IF ONLY . . .

Occasionally we all make bad decisions. Months or even years
later, we may still look back and think, *If only I'd taken that out-of-state
job! If only I'd finished college and gotten my degree! If only I'd waited
until I was married to have sexual relations!* Or, *Why didn't I think twice
before marrying an unbelieving spouse?*

Regrets sometimes have a sneaky way of lying dormant for long
periods of time and then resurfacing when we least expect them.
Emily was a twenty-seven-year-old married woman when she con-
sulted her doctor about her inability to get pregnant. The doctor
found that the problem stemmed from a botched abortion she'd had
in her late teens. She had desperately tried to forget that horrible time.
Now this secret from her past threatened her future. "My husband will

be devastated," she said. "He doesn't even know about the abortion. I don't know what to do."

Some regrets come from situations over which we've had little or no control. For Dawn, what seemed to be a good decision turned out to be a disaster because of a deliberate deception. "When I married Jim, I thought he was a solid Christian man. After the wedding, though, he suddenly refused to go to church and even resented it when I went without him. He had the nerve to blame me when he started seeing another woman. He lied to me from the very beginning."

> *Every loss leaves a space that can only be filled with God's presence.*
> —UNKNOWN

Then there was Carl, who foolishly and hastily entrusted the financial management of his paint and wallpaper business to a partner he barely knew. Over a six-month period, the partner methodically stole Carl's money, ruined his credit, and ultimately caused the doors to close on a business that had supported Carl and his family for fourteen years. His impulsive, misplaced trust came at a high cost and left him bitter and hesitant to trust his own instincts when it came to making a business or character judgment.

What do we do with our regrets? Are we destined to feel we are failures in certain areas of life? Or is there a productive way to deal with the missed opportunities, foolish mistakes, and the outright sin in our past? Not only is it important to deal with past regret; it's vital to understand the factors that led us to make poor decisions in the first place.

THE FEAR FACTOR

Have you ever listened to someone rationalize a decision he or she knew was wrong? Tracey was a young woman who was obviously going against her own standards when she said, "I know I shouldn't move in with my boyfriend, but I really love him. He says we need to find out if we're compatible before we make the commitment of marriage." It wasn't surprising when less than a year later the "live-in" arrangement ended and with it their relationship. Tracey's hurt was compounded by the regret of having compromised herself and her beliefs. At the time, however, her fear of losing her boyfriend dominated her better judgment.

Not all fear-based decisions are bad. When danger is near, fear is often a wise counselor and a strong ally. Think about coming upon a coiled rattlesnake, or smelling smoke in the middle of the night, or the sudden sense of alarm in the presence of a stranger. It is wise and reasonable in these situations to listen to your fears, and act upon them. But when fear rules your judgment outside the situation of an imminent threat, you may be making decisions you will eventually regret.

When we identify the fear that has prompted us to make a bad decision, we are a step closer to recognizing when a similar situation occurs in the future.

> *Faith is obedience at home and looking to the Master; obedience is faith going out to do his will.*
>
> —ANDREW MURRAY

Fears of rejection, failure, abandonment, or the unknown are all red flags if they are motivating a decision. Rather than quickly making a decision in the hopes of escaping these situations, we can take them to God and handle them as he has prescribed:

> *Do not be anxious about anything,*
> *but in everything, by prayer and petition,*
> *with thanksgiving, present your requests to God.*
> *And the peace of God, which transcends all understanding,*
> *will guard your hearts and your minds in Christ Jesus. (Phil. 4:6–7)*

People have been making fear-based decisions for thousands of years and often with harsh results. On three occasions Peter's fear led him to deny knowing Jesus. He feared that acknowledging a relationship with him would put him in personal danger. In the aftermath Peter may have been shocked by his own behavior, but Jesus was not. In fact, Jesus told Peter in advance of the exact time when his denials would occur. "'I tell you the truth,' Jesus answered, 'today—yes, tonight—before the rooster crows twice you yourself will disown me three times'"(Mark 14:30).

Later, following his third denial of Jesus, Peter heard the rooster crow for the second time. He recalled Jesus' words, and the Bible tells us that Peter broke down and wept (Mark 14:72). Peter had three opportunities to make the right decision, and each time fear overwhelmed his better judgment.

What good news that Peter's story doesn't end on this low and depressing note. Jesus loved Peter and knew his heart. In a touching act of forgiveness and restoration, the resurrected Jesus allowed Peter to speak out about his love for the Savior—not coincidentally—three times. As we follow Peter's life through the Scriptures, we see that he went on to become one of Jesus' most courageous, influential, and loyal followers.

THE SIN FACTOR

Fear is not the only factor that can push us into unwise decisions. Poor planning, impulsiveness, selfishness, immaturity, negative influences can put us on the road to regret.

Tracey, the young woman who decided to live with her boyfriend, was not only acting out of fear of rejection; she was also making a

> The only real mistake is one from which we learn nothing ... we must be patient with ourselves, just as God is infinitely patient with us.
> —JOHN POWELL

deliberate choice to do something she knew was wrong. This was sin, and she knew it. When we admit and agree with God that we have sinned, we have reached an important crossroads. We can either choose to remain in our sin, or with God's help we can turn away from the offensive behavior. Although Tracey suffered the consequences of her disobedience, her experience renewed her commitment to live according to her faith.

Not surprisingly, these times of realization are often intense and painful. Satan seizes the opportunity to jump in and tell us that our past mistakes have destroyed our future. He tries to convince us that our behavior is too shocking to bring before God—too shocking even to ask for forgiveness. Certainly, our heavenly Father is saddened by our sin, but he is not shocked. In Psalm 103, we read that God "knows how we are formed, he remembers we are dust" (v. 14). Our inner workings and inclinations are as familiar to God as the complex mechanisms of a watch are familiar to the watchmaker.

The Bible assures us that God not only forgives us of our sins when we confess them, he will also give us the strength we need to fight the temptation and avoid returning to our old ways (1 John 1:9; 1 Cor. 10:13).

THE FORGIVENESS FACTOR

If we are to leave the grip of sin and regret, we have to bring our attitudes and beliefs in line with God's truth and his will. Breaking with past sins is essential because many of our regrets result from following the world's ways rather than God's way. A great place to start is to ask God to reveal those areas in our life that need to be changed.

Search me, O God, and know my heart; test me and
know my anxious thoughts. See if there is any offensive way
in me, and lead me in the way everlasting. (Ps. 139:23–24)

As well as revealing our offensive ways, God can help us recognize the lies and deceit that are rooted in our beliefs. Once we see ourselves clearly in the light of God's truth, a wonderful thing happens—we become teachable. Left to our own inclinations, we may leap from the frying pan of our sinful thoughts and into the fire of stifling fret and self-condemnation. Regret and worry are similar in this way because worry is fretting about the future, while regret is fretting over the past.

> When God forgives he forgets. He buries our sin in the sea and puts a sign on the bank saying, "No Fishing Allowed."
> —CORRIE TEN BOOM

David, who authored seventy-three psalms, was a complex man who was well acquainted with sin and regret. In Psalm 103, he described the all-encompassing nature of God's forgiveness and compassion.

As far as the east is from the west,
so far has he removed our transgression from us. (Ps. 103:12)

If we were to set out traveling due north, our journey would ultimately take us to the North Pole. If we continued on in the same direction, we would eventually find ourselves traveling south. The poles define north and south. However, if we set about traveling east, we could travel endlessly in that direction, never reaching west. As the saying goes, "East is east and west is west, and never the twain shall meet." God, in extravagant forgiveness, has made sure that a repentant believer and his forgiven sin will never meet. Breaking free of the bondage of circular, condemning thoughts can begin when we confidently accept God's forgiveness.

THE PRIZE OF PEACE

When we grasp the liberating truth of God's forgiveness, we can begin to break the pattern of wayward thoughts by washing our minds through meditating on God's Word. No longer are we hopelessly ensnared in the world's ways and thoughts; we can begin the process of renewing our heart and mind. It's not enough to avoid our old thought patterns; we must replace our old thoughts with new thoughts.

Do not conform any longer to the pattern of this world,
but be transformed by the renewing of your mind.
Then you will be able to test and approve what God's will is—
his good, pleasing and perfect will. (Rom. 12:2)

The benefit of obediently washing our mind with these thoughts is no less than the promise of the peace and the presence of God in our lives.

Finally, brothers, whatever is true, whatever is noble,
whatever is right, whatever is pure, whatever is lovely, whatever
is admirable—if anything is excellent or praiseworthy—think
about such things. Whatever you have learned or received or
heard from me, or seen in me—put it into practice. And the
God of peace will be with you. (Phil. 4:8–9)

This radical shift breaks the chains of mental impurity to the freedom of thinking with the mind of Christ. It's helpful to remember that it was Paul who penned these verses. If God can fulfill the promise of transformation in Paul, whose mission had once been to wipe out the Christian faith, He can also fulfill it in every person who diligently seeks it.

Dealing with regret doesn't mean glossing over the past or allowing it to become a stumbling block to the future. It means that we recognize it for what it is, learn from it, and trust God to lead us forward. Paul could have wasted his life fretting over his actions toward the church, but instead, God enabled him to leave his past behind him and devote himself to serving the very ones he once sought to destroy.

Brothers, I do not consider myself yet to have taken hold of it. But one thing I do: Forgetting what is behind and straining toward what is ahead, I press on toward the goal to win the prize for which God has called me heavenward in Christ Jesus. (Phil. 3:13–14)

Is there life after regret? Yes, most definitely. We serve a God who promises to cause all things to work together for good to those who love him, to those who are called according to his purpose (see Rom. 8:28). God can take the very source of our brokenness and use it to make us whole. Knowing this, we can thank our sovereign God and press on.

SUNDOWN

"I'm not coming home on Friday, Dad!" Vicki brushed away her tears with the back of her hand.

"You'll do what I say!" His voice was barely under control. He looked around to see if any customers were within hearing range.

She continued pushing her point. "I think it's ridiculous to come home for two weeks and then turn right around and go back again! Why can't I just stay there?"

> *And we know that God causes all things to work together for good to those who love God, to those who are called according to His purpose.*
> —ROMANS 8:28
> (NASB)

"We've been over this. I want you to drive up with your brother and cousin, find an apartment near the campus, give them a deposit to hold it, and be home by Friday." He grabbed a rag from his back pocket and angrily rubbed his greasy hands. "I do have something to say in this, Vicki. Who do you think is paying for your tuition and your apartment?"

"I know. But, Dad . . . ."

A customer had finished filling up his tank and was digging in his wallet as he approached the office.

In a harsh whisper her father said, "It's settled, Victoria! Find an apartment and then come home. You can go back up on the weekend before the semester starts but not a day before. Do you understand?"

Vicki stared into his eyes but said nothing. Yes, she knew she would have to come back, but she wasn't about to give him the satisfaction of hearing her say it.

He stepped behind the cash register. "Now, go on. I don't want you kids driving in the dark."

Once in the backseat of the car, Vicki's full anger erupted. "I can't wait to be on my own! I don't know why he even wants me to come back home. Since Mom died, he hardly says a word to me. He just gets up and goes to work, and comes home and goes to bed. What does it matter whether I'm there or not?"

Phil looked at her from the front seat. "You know how he is, Vic. He's never talked to us very much—even before Mom got cancer. He's just not the kind to show his feelings."

"Oh, I don't know. I think he shows his feelings pretty well," Vicki said. "I just don't think he can stand being around me!"

Jeremy cocked his head toward her. "You know, my dad's the same way. He's really quiet until it comes time to lower the boom on us kids. Then it all breaks loose, and we can't wait until he's quiet again!" He laughed and shrugged his shoulders. "It must be the way they were raised. I think their parents were pretty cold."

"Vic," said Phil, "you've got to admit that you haven't been the easiest person in the world to get along with lately. Anytime Dad wants to go somewhere with you or do something as a family, you always manage to weasel out of it."

"Yeah, I know," said Vicki. Her tone softened. "I've been feeling bad about that. It's ironic because ever since last year when I became a Christian, I've really wanted to talk to him—you know—seriously, but it seems like whenever we try, we end up fighting. It's just easier to avoid him."

They had been on the road for a couple of hours when Jeremy glanced into the rearview mirror and saw flashing red lights. "Oh, man! A cop! I'm getting busted, and I wasn't even speeding!"

He pulled over, rolled down the window, and watched in his side mirror as the officer approached the car. After handing him his license and insurance papers, the officer asked Jeremy to walk with him to the patrol car.

Phil and Vicki watched out the rear window. The officer wasn't writing a ticket, but he was talking intently to Jeremy.

"Something's not right," said Phil.

Jeremy got back in the car and fastened his seat belt. His voice was somber. "We have to go back." He turned the car toward home.

Vicki felt a wave of nausea.

Somehow Phil and Vicki already knew that something terrible had happened to their dad, but neither of them could bring themselves to ask. It was as if they had picked up an invisible hitchhiker who dominated the conversation with unspoken dread.

The last of sunset's coral-colored clouds succumbed to darkness as they pulled up to their house. The police were there, and Uncle John's car was in the driveway. Their Dad's car was no where to be seen.

Vicki and Phil learned that the unthinkable had happened. Their dad had been lying on his back on a "creeper" under the motor home he was repairing. His helper got into the vehicle to start up the engine when it suddenly lurched and ran over their father, killing him instantly.

That was seventeen years ago.

Vicki knows that, the moment she asked, God forgave her anger and the harsh words spoken to her father on that fateful day. Learning to forgive herself, however, has been a much longer process. Dealing with the grief and the profound regret of that day was compounded by the unexpressed and delayed grief for her mother's death. Gradually Vicki was able to gain perspective on these events, but in many ways they have shaped her life and the lives of her husband and their five children.

The Bible says, "'In your anger do not sin:' Do not let the sun go down while you are still angry" (Eph. 4:26). This verse has become a guiding life verse for Vicki and for her family.

The kids know that if they argue with one another they have to reach some kind of resolution before they go to bed. The same goes for Vicki and her husband. If they have cross words with each other or with the kids, they too, make it a point to end the day on a peaceful, loving note.

Whether leaving the house for school, a business trip, or the grocery store, Vicki and her family always try to make their parting words those of love and kindness. It's a joyful habit born out of sad experience. Vicki doesn't think of her actions as paranoid; instead, she sees them as conscious evidence that she has learned from her mistakes and no longer takes the people she loves for granted. She knows there's no way to change the past, but she can, and does, treasure the present.

Forget Me Not

When they met, James was nineteen, and Lisa was fifteen. He was unlike any boy she'd ever known—worldly, handsome, and surrounded with an aura of danger and rebellion that both frightened and compelled her.

Lisa had been raised in a Christian home, and her values reflected her upbringing. She tried to live a godly life, and her special, private goal was to remain pure until she married. James realized immediately that Lisa's faith was important to her. When he told her that he had been curious about religion and wanted to go to church, Lisa felt that his interest somehow sanctioned the relationship. They began dating. It soon became clear that James didn't have church on his mind. By that time, however, the relationship had a momentum of its own.

James was consumed with her and jealous of anyone or anything that took her away from him. Before long, Lisa was estranged from her friends and had withdrawn from nearly all of her school activities.

One night when they were alone, things went too far. In a split second Lisa's dream of remaining pure for her future husband was shattered. Guilt and sadness plagued her, but the intimate relationship continued over the next year. Once when she tried to break up with him, he made a superficial attempt to kill himself. She got the message; she couldn't leave him.

When her senior year started, she was growing more and more resentful of the way James dominated her life. She had been looking forward to her last year of soccer and all the special functions of her senior year, but she had to remain on the fringes in order to please James. Privately she looked forward to going away to college. Hopefully it would bring their relationship to a natural conclusion. Those hopes vanished when Lisa realized she was pregnant.

James wanted to marry her, but Lisa wouldn't consider it. She thought about turning to her parents, but they were prominent in the community. This would break their hearts and publicly embarrass them. Finally, she confided in a friend who went with her to a women's clinic downtown. The counselor talked with Lisa and ultimately advised an abortion, saying that under the circumstances it was the "right thing to do."

The abortion was scheduled immediately because Lisa was already eight weeks along. During the brief counseling session, the procedure had been discussed so passively that the physical pain of it came as a complete shock to Lisa. Afterwards, in an atmosphere of resigned silence, she dressed to return home and silently recover and cope on her own.

In order to cope Lisa immediately broke up with James. After what she had been through, his vague threats had lost their power. All she wanted was to get as far away from him as possible and blot these terrible events from her memory.

The next few years were a blur of drinking and partying punctuated by excessive sleep. James was out of her life, but her new relationships with men somehow took on the same unhealthy and controlling characteristics. Deep inside she believed that must be all she deserved.

One day as she was driving to work, she noticed a crowd of protesters outside an abortion clinic. She looked away and turned up the radio. She didn't want to hear their chants or read their signs. She would make sure to go home by a different route.

But a few days later, the subject came up again—this time on the car radio. Recently Lisa had been listening to Dr. James Dobson's radio program *Focus on the Family*. Today the discussion was about healing for women who'd had abortions. Lisa reached for the radio dial but then realized there was not a hint of condemnation in their voices, just compassion. They discussed the deep emotional pain caused by abortion and the resulting feeling of being separated from God. Lisa nodded her head; she knew exactly what they meant. She sat in her car to listen to the conclusion of the program.

Once inside her apartment Lisa fell across her bed and, for the first time in years, wept for her aborted baby. She prayed for God's forgiveness—not just for the abortion but also for the premarital sex that led her to it. Little by little her life began to change. She couldn't undo the past, but she was committed to living each new day to please God.

Lisa met a wonderful man and eventually they began discussing marriage. She knew she had to tell him about the abortion. She braced herself for the possibility that he might reject her. Instead he held her reassuringly and said, "I'm so sorry, Lisa. We can talk more about it, or we don't have to—whatever you want."

They were married. After their first child was born, Lisa's unresolved grief over the abortion resurfaced. She searched for books to help her deal with the delayed trauma she was experiencing. Although she found a couple of books, it was just too difficult to confront the issues alone.

Their daughter was just six months old when Lisa suspected she might be pregnant again. She had heard about a Christian organization called the Crisis Pregnancy Center that provided free pregnancy tests. At the Center the intake form included a question that asked if she'd ever had an abortion. She answered yes and was referred to an organization called HEART—an acronym for Healing Encouragement for Abortion-Related Trauma.

When she was six months pregnant with her second child, Lisa went through the program. After years of feeling isolated by her past experience, she was comforted to be among other women who were dealing with the same issue. As the women shared their stories, Lisa recognized that she had experienced a predictable pattern of anger, depression, and guilt.

She had spent years trying not to think about the baby that would never be, but the program encouraged just the opposite. As part of the process of letting go of the unresolved issues surrounding the abortion, Lisa wrote a letter to her baby. A special memorial service was given to honor and consecrate the baby's memory. For this service Lisa found a picture of a toddler wearing a large hat and standing on the beach looking out over the ocean. The child's back was to the camera. Under the picture were the words, "forget me not"—Lisa knew she never would. At long last she released her baby to the Lord and began the process of healing and acceptance.

The effect of this process on Lisa was profound. Following the birth of her second child, she went through the program again to deal with lingering issues such as telling her parents and her children.

Eventually she began speaking to groups in various churches, telling them about her experience and the peace that she found in God through the help of HEART. Now Lisa is the director of HEART through the Pregnancy Resource Centers of Greater Portland. She knows the best way to avoid the regret she has experienced is to help women see other solutions to a problem pregnancy. For those who are living with guilt and regret from a past abortion, she prays that she can help them find the freedom of forgiveness that only God can give.

THE OTHER SIDE OF THE FENCE

They lay side by side in the darkness.

"I'm just not happy anymore," Tony said.

"But, honey," said Donna, "you've felt this way before, and we got through it. Maybe it's just another phase you're going through." She turned on the lamp and looked at him. "We have a good marriage and four great kids." Her voice broke with emotion. "Don't throw our life away to chase after some nonexistent rainbow!"

He turned his face to the wall. "I just don't know. I wish things were like they used to be when we were first married. Life was exciting and romantic."

"Tony, things change—they have to—they should! We're not newlyweds anymore, and we haven't been for twenty-two years. We have lots of responsibilities, but lots of blessings, too. Can't you be thankful for what you have?"

Lately Tony hadn't been thinking much about what he had. Instead, everywhere he turned, he only saw what he didn't have and what he desperately wanted. He wasn't ready to passively accept a life of less than the best, and he certainly wasn't ready to fade quietly into the sunset! At forty-four, he was still vital, young, and alive! At work he was just hitting his stride—when he came into a meeting, all eyes were on him. His opinion was held in high regard. He felt respected, powerful, and successful. When he walked by the secretaries, he knew they were watching and admiring him. He loved the way he felt when he received a warm smile or a lingering glance.

But when he walked into his own home, he felt no such excitement or intrigue. Instead, the kids pounced on him; his wife gave him a peck on the cheek and then put him to work doing mundane and meaningless chores. More and more often he put off coming directly home by arranging to meet with friends for a drink after work. All he had to tell Donna was that he had "an appointment." She never questioned him or seemed to doubt him. Maybe she thought if she ignored it, it would pass like it had last time.

Donna was right when she said they had gone through this before. Several years ago, there had been a time when he felt neglected and restless in their marriage. When he told her how he felt, she had gone out of her way to pay attention to him and spend time with him. They even saw a marriage counselor. For a while they seemed to be more conscious and aware of each other's needs, but as the crisis evened out, they fell back into their old familiar ways.

She was doing it again—taking him for granted! It was true that she was an excellent mother to the kids, but he had needs, too—a fact to which she seemed blinded. Now when she suggested that they see their pastor or a marriage counselor, he flatly rejected the idea, saying, "We've tried that before, and, obviously, it didn't help because here we are still dealing with the very same problems."

Sometimes he would purposefully try to pick a fight by provoking her with cruel statements. He even attacked her personally. "You don't even care enough to keep yourself slim and fit for me." Deep down he knew her appearance wasn't really the problem, but somehow, fighting with her was better than settling for the stagnate status quo. Although he could see that she was angry and hurt, she never countered his insults with hateful words of her own. Most often she retreated to the bedroom in tears. He hated that most of all!

When a business trip to San Francisco came up, he looked forward to being away for several days, but Donna was filled with apprehension. She tearfully walked him to the door. "Do you really have to go?" she said. "I think it's important that we're not separated right now. Won't you reconsider asking Mom to come stay with the kids so I can go with you?"

He hated her pleading. "This is hardly a separation, Donna," he said. "I have to go. It's a business trip, not a vacation!"

On some level Donna must have known it was more than a simple business trip, and it was. Tony had long admired a woman named Leah who worked for the same company in the San Francisco office. On this trip, his discontent at home was all the justification he needed to begin an affair with her.

A few months later when the company offered him a promotion and transfer to the San Francisco office, he took it without hesitation. He made it clear to Donna that he had no intention of taking his family with him. She begged him to stay and work to save their marriage, but he resolutely packed his belongings. Before he left, he filed for divorce.

In the ultimate irony, only a couple of months after the divorce was final, Tony began to think about Donna and miss her and the life they'd had together. It's true that his life was no longer boring, but it didn't take long for him to realize that Leah was not someone he wanted to spend his life with. In fact she couldn't hold a candle to Donna.

Whenever he called the house, Donna was kind but cool as she put the kids on the phone to talk with him. She always cooperated in arranging his visits with the children, but if he tried to initiate an ordinary conversation with her, she said she had to go and hung up.

About a year and a half later, he saw his ex-wife at the wedding of their niece. Donna was positively radiant that day in a pink chiffon dress and a wide-brimmed hat. The kids and family seemed magnetized to her as she laughed and smiled in her warm and easy way. Tony couldn't take his eyes off her.

At the reception he calculated a moment alone with her and cautiously came up beside her. "Hello, Donna," he said. "You look terrific."

"Thank you," she said.

He decided to jump right in. "I've been thinking about you a lot—you and the kids, that is."

She looked at him blankly.

"You know, Donna, I've been a complete jerk. I know this must seem . . . ."

Donna began to fidget uncomfortably and glance around the room.

He'd started down this path, so he pressed on. "I know this seems crazy, but do you think you could ever consider, even remotely . . . ."

She suddenly waved at someone behind him. "Over here, Jack!"

Tony was in a daze as Donna linked her arm through Jack's and said, "Jack, this is the kids' dad, Tony."

Jack extended his hand, and Tony mechanically met it with his own.

"Tony, this is Jack Harrison, my fiancé."

The realities crashed home with a tragic force. He saw with stunning clarity that for years he had been in total control of his relationship with Donna, and with only the slightest effort he could have turned it around and kept the wonderful thing he had. Now he was powerless to change a thing. It was too late.

Eventually, Tony too remarried, but it was over almost before it began. Afterwards, he drifted into a long period of heavy drinking and an empty succession of women who only magnified his loneliness and the loss he constantly felt.

Today, Tony's doing his best to put his life back together and rebuild the fractured relationships with his kids. It's harder now because once Donna and Jack married, they moved several states away. Tony's going to church again and trying to live a good life, but he's still haunted by the knowledge that he carelessly threw away what he'd really wanted all along. He had convinced himself that there was greener grass out there somewhere—he was wrong. If only he hadn't been so prideful and cocky; if only he had realized sooner what a good thing he'd had; if only . . . .

◆ ◆

LOOKING BACK ON LESSONS LEARNED

- Regrets can come from a variety of sources: making bad decisions, following the ways of the world, succumbing to sin, or being innocently hurt or misled by another. Until we deal with them, regrets can haunt us and dictate the course of our lives.

- Regret is fretting about the past while worry is fretting about the future.

- Fear-based decisions often become our deepest regrets. If we find ourselves justifying or rationalizing a decision, we may be on the brink of doing something we will eventually regret.

- Satan loves to tell us that our past mistakes have ruined our future, but God says no such thing. The apostle Peter's life is a sweet reassurance that failure doesn't mean that God won't use us again.

- Once we have sincerely sought out his forgiveness, God will never browbeat us with old mistakes.

- The apostle Paul said, "Whatever is noble, whatever is right, whatever is pure, whatever is lovely, whatever is admirable—if anything is excellent or praiseworthy—think about such things" (Phil. 4:8). When we avoid recriminating thought patterns and replace them with new ones, the result will be peace of mind.

- Amazingly, God can take the very source of our brokenness and use it to make us whole.

- A past regret can become a beacon that helps us stay on course.

- Dealing with the regret doesn't mean glossing over the past, nor does it mean dwelling on it and allowing it to become a stumbling block to the future. We must recognize our mistakes, learn from them, and trust God to lead us forward.

10

Following in Your Father's Footsteps

> *"Behold, I stand at the door and knock. If anyone
> hears My voice and opens the door, I will come
> in to him and dine with him, and he with Me.*
> REVELATION 3:20 NKJV

Life had not been easy for Debi. As a child, the ongoing abuse and estrangement at home had prompted her to look for love elsewhere. When she was very young, she was involved with a boy and got pregnant. Because of her religious training, Debi knew this kind of intimacy was prohibited outside of marriage, so even after she and the father married, the coming baby felt less like a blessing than proof of her sin. When little Teri arrived, Debi's ambivalent feelings persisted, and she regarded her baby girl with aloof resentment.

Just over a year later, a son arrived—Joey. The baby boy had a mysterious handicap that manifested in retardation and severe seizures, but her son melted Debi's hardened heart, and for the first time in her life, she felt love.

The marriage ended after three years, and Debi went to work to support her children. Because Joey's problems required specialized twenty-four-hour care and expensive medication that Debi couldn't afford, she had to make the wrenching decision to place him in a foster home. She hoped she could earn enough money to eventually bring him home, but after a time in foster care, she had reached a point when she was forced to make the decision either to take him back permanently or sign papers that made Joey a ward of the state.

Debi sat on the living room floor and cried while writing down her thoughts. Her circumstances wouldn't allow her to keep her son, but it broke her heart. Joey was home for a visit. She listened to the children laughing and playing in the bedroom. Never again would she experience this simple joy. When he was a ward of the state, he would not be allowed to come home.

Despair overwhelmed her. She reread her writing and was only mildly surprised to realize she had been writing a good-bye letter to her children. It seemed to make sense. She would escape her pain, and they would probably be better off without her.

In tears, she knelt to pray but couldn't. Debi had been exposed to Christian teaching all her life, but it had been coupled with abuse from both of her parents. Her father had been physically abusive and controlling; her mother had been verbally abusive, disinterested, and neglectful. Although she often had heard that Jesus loved her and wanted to be Lord of her life, Debi saw religion as contradictory and confusing. Now, in this most difficult time, she had nowhere to turn.

A sharp knock on the door roused Debi from her thoughts. Wiping her swollen eyes, she stood up to answer it. She opened the door. No one was there. Stepping out on the porch she looked around. *Probably the neighbor kids*, she thought. She returned to the living room floor and continued writing. The knocking came again. Now she was irritated, and from her place on the floor she called out, "Who is it?"

What she heard next would change her life forever.

"Deborah, it's me, Jesus. This is the last time I will knock."

Debi sat in stunned silence. She knew instantly that this was not a religion or a "belief system" calling to her; it was a Person—Jesus—God! And he was calling to her personally.

Unlike the many occasions before when she had ignored his call, this time Debi eagerly answered that knock on the door of her heart. There on her living room floor, she prayed to receive Christ as her Lord and Savior.

Debi's life did not suddenly become problem-free. In fact, her greatest challenge lay ahead as she parted with her precious Joey, but God gave her the strength to do what she needed to do. Although the difficult decision was made about Joey, God was just beginning in the lives of Debi and her little girl, Teri.

Debi's hardships were exceptionally severe, but we all share the common experience of living in a troubled and searching society. A stroll through the aisles of a bookstore will confirm the magnitude of the quest for that elusive missing piece of our lives. St. Augustine saw God's plan and man's dilemma when he said, "Thou hast formed us for thyself, and our hearts are restless till they find rest in thee."

A popular child's toy is a plastic sphere with holes cut in the shapes of a circle, triangle, square, etc. The purpose of the toy is for the toddler to find the square-shaped piece and put it in the square-shaped hole, the round piece in the round hole, and so on. Invariably, the child first tries to fit a wrong shape into the hole. However, regardless of how he pounds and maneuvers, the hole will only accept the piece of the same shape. Similarly, each person has a God-shaped hole in his heart. No matter how we try

> *He who abandons himself to God will never be abandoned by God.*
> —UNKNOWN

to pound other things into this space—a job, house, car, other beliefs or philosophies—nothing will fill that void until we seek God and allow him to perfectly occupy our hearts.

Maybe you have made a succession of hapless decisions in the hope of filling a nameless yearning. Stop striving, back up, and put a firm foundation under your life. You can't build a future—much less an eternity—on anything less solid than a total commitment to Jesus Christ.

If you find yourself in the position of uncertainty about your spiritual walk and beliefs, it may help to think about the following guideposts. Perhaps you will find both the missing *piece* and the missing *peace* you've been searching for.

CHOOSE LIFE

You may hold an intellectual belief in Jesus. Perhaps you accept that he was an actual historical figure who did noteworthy things and led an exemplary life. In spite of this, however, you still feel empty. Oddly, that emptiness is a blessing. God loves you so much that he won't let you be satisfied with a two-dimensional understanding of Christ or anything less than a *genuine* relationship with him. In the Bible, James points out that belief alone is not enough.

You believe that there is one God. Good!
Even the demons believe that—and shudder. (James 2:19)

Believing in the existence of Jesus is only the beginning. What do you do with that belief? Belief must be accompanied by the choice to bring God into your life and allow him to lead you. Choice is an active, conscious process, and without it, there is neither growth nor change.

Sarah appeared to be an average middle-aged woman, but she lived a life of quiet desperation. Over and over her expectations were failed. Nothing was terribly wrong, but nothing was truly right. She struggled constantly with depression and fear. On these "dark days" she fell into a nameless, shapeless despair. Each glance into the mirror confirmed the passage of time, and with each passing day there seemed to be fewer possibilities and less hope. For years she'd found comfort in marijuana, but even that was failing her lately. Now, instead of feeling creative and energized, she just felt dull and tired.

> He who consciously or unconsciously has chosen to ignore God is an orphan in the universe.
> —EMILE CAILLIET

In college she discovered she could write poetry. Her English professor was so enthusiastic about her talent that he suggested she might one day be published. She was thrilled, but somehow, outside of the classroom, she lacked the discipline to focus her energies and hone her raw talent. On a few occasions she sent her work to literary magazines, but if she received a rejection letter, she crumpled her work and threw it into the wastebasket.

When she was particularly low, she phoned her sister. Although she loved Winnie, she got tired of hearing the same old thing from her: "Sarah, you need God in your life."

Sarah believed that Jesus had lived, but if he was still alive as Winnie said, he didn't seem very interested in her. After all, she'd prayed after their mother had died, but nothing had happened.

Religion was a good thing for Winnie, but apparently it just "didn't take" for her.

Sarah is living under a common and dangerous misconception. She mistakenly thinks that belief aimlessly alights like a butterfly on some people and simply floats by others. What is missing from this point of view is personal *choice*. The necessity of making a definite choice to love and serve God was confirmed by many of the Old Testament writers.

> But if serving the LORD seems undesirable to you,
> then **choose for yourselves** this day whom you will serve...
> But as for me and my household,
> we will serve the LORD. (Josh. 24:15, emphasis added)
> I have set before you life and death, blessings and curses.
> Now **choose life**, so that you and your children may live and
> that you may love the LORD your God, listen to his voice,
> and hold fast to him. (Deut. 30:19, emphasis added)

"Choose," "listen," "hold fast"—these are not passive words. It's likely that at one time Sarah received a strong prompting from the Lord, but like her expectation to be a successful poet simply because she had talent, she also expected to have belief bestowed on her (see Rom. 10:9–10). She refused to recognize that she had a role and a determining choice in the matter.

God is a Gentleman; he would never bully his way into a life. We are involved, and each person must make the choice to confess that Jesus is Lord and receive him into his or her heart.

CHOOSE FAITH

How do we trust in a God we cannot see? Faith is cultivated by hearing the Word of God, believing the Word of God, and putting the Word of God into practice. The power of faith is in Christ, so our faith is not simply in faith; it is in the Savior. When we trust the facts of Scripture, faith will follow, and eventually feelings of peace and joy.

> Now faith is being sure of what we hope for and
> certain of what we do not see. (Heb. 11:1)

Trusting God means letting go of walking through life based strictly by sight. Living beyond that which we can see challenges a deep sense of security. Like a novice swinging from a trapeze, it takes courage to unclasp your grip in the hope that you'll be caught in the arms of Jesus. Don't fear. Not only will he be there to catch you; he's the net that stretches beneath you!

Trust in the LORD with all your heart and lean not on your own understanding; in all your ways acknowledge him, and he will make your paths straight. Do not be wise in your own eyes. (Prov. 3:5-7)

Making the decision to submit your will to the will of God demonstrates a trusting heart in the hands of worthy-of-trust God.

CHOOSE LOVE

We can have a head full of Bible knowledge and still have a desolate heart that is empty of God. Until we have chosen to love God unreservedly with our whole being, our Christian walk will be confusing, frustrating, and ineffective. Jesus made clear the total commitment he requires when he told us the greatest commandment:

"'Love the Lord your God with all your heart and with all your soul and with all your mind and with all your strength.'

The second is this: 'Love your neighbor as yourself.'

There is no commandment greater than these" (Mark 12:30–31).

Our heart, soul, mind, and strength represent our total physical and spiritual selves. Therefore, loving God is a free-will decision that involves surrendering our deepest emotions, the use and agreement of our minds, and harnessing our bodily strength to serve God in an all-encompassing relationship. God does not want to be relegated to a corner of our life. He requires it *all*.

In the absence of any other proof, the thumb alone would convince me of God's existence.
—SIR ISAAC NEWTON

Debi's decision to receive Christ gave her the faith and strength to sign the papers that made little Joey a ward of the state and ensured that he would have the proper medical care. Sadly, two years later Joey suffered a massive seizure and died at the age of three.

Grief threatened Debi's sanity to the point that she could no longer care for her daughter. She faced the truth that she had always deprived

Teri of the love she deserved. To her horror, she suspected she was repeating the same neglectful abuse with her little girl that she had experienced from her own mother. The decision was made for her daughter to stay with relatives for a while.

Debi kept in close contact with Teri, and slowly, visit by visit, a long-awaited love began to evolve for her daughter. However, she still doubted her ability to care for her the way that she should.

> *Those who live in the Lord never see each other for the last time.*
> —UNKNOWN

Months passed. On Mother's Day Debi sat in church and listened to a message about the value of a godly mother. She stared at a little girl sitting across the aisle who had black hair and deep brown eyes like Teri. Tears fell onto her lap as she prayed, "God, please give me another chance to be a mommy."

And he did. It was not always easy. There were times when the arguments were so intense between Debi and her daughter that they both went to their rooms for "time out." But they were managing, and they were happier.

One September day as Debi and Teri were driving home from the grocery store, Teri asked, "Momma, you never used to love me, and now you do. How come?"

Debi was shaken. They had never talked about her early lack of love for her daughter. In fact, Debi had prayed that her feelings of resentment and the resulting neglect would be blocked from Teri's memory. But they weren't.

Debi pulled over to the side of the road and took her daughter in her arms. She told her about Jesus and how he changed her life making it possible for her to love.

Teri listened intently. "Momma, do I have to wait until I'm old like you, or can I accept Jesus now?"

Debi led Teri in her decision to receive Christ. Teri is twenty-one now, and she and her mother are the best of friends. Without God, Debi believes she never would have been able to break the cycle of abuse and build the wonderful relationship she has with her daughter.

There will always be a hole in Debi's heart for Joey, but she relies on the fact that they will be together one day. In his short little life, Joey accomplished a great deal. He taught his troubled mother how to love and led her into the everlasting arms of the Savior.

CHOOSE NOW!

The simple trust and faith that Teri demonstrated when she asked her mother if she, too, could receive Christ have proven to be obstacles for many individuals. "It can't be that easy," they reason. "There must be more to it than praying a simple prayer." The Bible, however, tells us:

> That if you confess with your mouth, "Jesus is Lord,"
> and believe in your heart that God raised him from the dead,
> you will be saved. (Rom. 10:9)

The glorious truth is that the simple decision to receive Jesus is a step through a narrow doorway that leads to a wide, deep, and profoundly rewarding life.

Maybe God is knocking on the door of your heart right now. If you haven't yet opened that door and invited him in, do it now by praying this prayer:

Heavenly Father,

> I've gone my own way, Lord, and I know that I am a
> sinner. Forgive me, and help me to turn away from my
> sins. I want to answer the knock on the door of my heart.
> Come into my life and be my Lord and my Savior.
>
> In Jesus' name, amen.

The most important decision a person can make is the decision to follow Jesus Christ. Once this heartfelt choice is made, we have not only changed our eternity; we have entered a new dimension of life.

> And this is the testimony: God has given us eternal life,
> and this life is in his Son. He who has the Son has life;
> he who does not have the Son of God does not have life.
> (1 John 5:11–12)

No longer must we "go it alone" when we confront the cares and confusion of the world. Now we have an awesome God whose will and guidance are available to us through his Word and through prayer. In this chapter we will read how others have reached the moment of spiritual commitment and how that decision has changed their lives.

SUSAN'S QUEST

Susan's spiritual journey began in high school when she went to church one evening with some friends. Although she really didn't understand what it meant, she responded to an altar call. There was no change in her life, but she was content to let the unresolved issues lie dormant.

Salvation is not turning over a new leaf but receiving a new life.
—UNKNOWN

Her interest resurfaced in college when she enrolled in a comparative religions class. She was captivated by all the different ideas and complex philosophies. That fascination led her in the opposite direction of believing there was one truth. Christianity, in contrast, seemed almost too simple.

While in college Susan met Dean. They fell in love and were married after they graduated. Dean was a Christian, and she thought that was fine—for him. For Susan, the New Age concepts were becoming increasingly appealing. She especially liked the fact that New Age embraced any number of ideas and philosophies, which meant that she could create her own mix of whatever she chose to believe, including transcendental meditation and Buddhism. The concepts of reincarnation, higher consciousness, and Nirvana seemed a logical explanation of the way the world worked. Reincarnation and karma supported a cause-and-effect system in which the quality of the next life was determined by life and behavior in this life. If a person was horrible and selfish, he would have a terrible life; if he was kind and generous, he would have a good life. It seemed to make sense.

When their first daughter, Jenny, was born, Susan and Dean decided to start attending church on a regular basis. Although they were both involved in church, Susan was also attending a Buddhist group where the emphasis was on meditation, auras, and the use of crystals in healing.

Eventually, having one foot in Christianity and the other in New Age beliefs raised some problems. For one thing, the other beliefs were not only contradictory to biblical teaching; they were antagonistic toward it. At one point Susan went to the meditation leader and talked with her about Christianity's basic tenet that Christ died for our sins. The leader looked at Susan squarely, "Surely you don't believe that someone else's death could have any effect on your sins." That was the end of the discussion.

Susan knew something was missing from her life, but she couldn't figure out what it was. By now she had heard the gospel many times, and while she could easily see the wisdom in the Bible, the logic escaped her. For two years she had been attending a morning Bible study group. Eventually she felt safe enough to begin asking questions.

"This just doesn't make sense to me," she said one day. "I don't see how someone else can die for my sins. And why is the Old Testament full of stories about sacrifice? It seems so gruesome and cruel. Why should a sacrifice be necessary in order to worship God?"

Although no one fully answered her questions, a friend told her about a woman named Rosie who was especially good at dealing with these kinds of issues. It turned out that Rosie was going to be at a women's retreat that was coming up in a few months. For that reason, Susan planned to go.

Soon Susan's life took a turn that caused her questioning to take on a new urgency and importance. During a treadmill test for a routine physical, Dean's heart stopped, and he was taken to the coronary care unit. During an angiogram procedure, his heart stopped again. He was quickly revived, but no solid answers could explain the two episodes.

Susan was stunned that her young husband could have this kind of problem. Dean was baffled by his sudden health problems, too, but he was secure and peaceful. "If I die, I know where I'm going," he said calmly.

Peace was the last thing Susan felt. At home alone with their two little girls, she contemplated an unknown future. Where could she turn for comfort? She phoned her dad who did his best to reassure her. As they ended the conversation, he asked, "Honey, do you have something to help you sleep?"

His question echoed the deeper question resonating in her soul: *Do I have something to help me with life—and death?* The answer came like a dull thud: *No—nothing*. No amount of interesting ideas, relaxation methods, or aspirations to higher consciousness could compensate for the total lack of love, comfort, and hope she felt.

As it turned out, Dean fully recovered from his ordeal, though no definitive cause for his problem was found. Normal life resumed. Oddly, Susan's Bible reading was becoming more regular and more meaningful. Every now and then, a verse would seem to pop off the page and speak to her. One day in her reading, she came across Jesus' saying that a house divided against itself cannot stand (Mark 3:25). For the first time she could see that her scattered beliefs had made her a fragile and unstable person.

The women's retreat came about four-and-a-half months after Dean's heart problem. As she had hoped, she met with Rosie and asked the questions that had been troubling her. Rather than voicing her own opinions and experiences, Rosie opened the Bible and showed her the Scriptures that explained them. They talked about the meaning of the Old Testament animal sacrifices—how God had instituted them as far back as Adam and Eve as the means of covering our sins and allowing us to come into God's presence. One by one they read the Old Testament verses. To Susan's surprise she could see that instead of a bloodthirsty God who required the senseless death of animals, he had lovingly provided a way for sinful man to reach Holy God through the purity of the sacrifices. By the time they worked their way into the New Testament, the fog was lifting from Susan's heart. She finally understood that Christ's sacrificial death on the cross was the once-and-for-all solution to mankind's separation from God.

It was after midnight when she and Rosie finished talking. "Susan," Rosie said, "now you need to choose to give your life to Christ. This is a life or death decision, and you need to make it now."

Alone that night, Susan pondered her words. Since Dean's problem with his heart, life-and-death had taken on new meaning. Her tears seemed to come from a place deep inside. Not only did she finally see herself as a sinner who needed God's grace and forgiveness; she realized how she hungered for the unconditional love of God through Jesus. It was time to make a choice. She chose Jesus.

"Lord," she prayed, "I still don't understand everything, but you just teach me as you want me to learn."

She knew he was there and had heard her prayer. There was such relief in letting go of all the unknowns. The lonely and frustrating search was over.

Now, fifteen years later, the Bible has never failed to fascinate and compel her. Christianity once seemed too simple, but the more she studies, the more she understands that she could never totally explore its depths. Susan no longer holds an eclectic blend of intellectual ideas and theories. Instead she holds fast to a Person—Jesus.

Body and Soul

Janine sat in the waiting room at the county health department and fidgeted with the zipper on her purse. She glanced around the room. A pregnant woman flipped through a magazine, an older woman wrote in a small notebook, and a young mother hovered over her new baby in its infant carrier.

Janine felt self-conscious and conspicuous. Was it obvious to everyone why she was here? Her relief to be out of the waiting room and in an examining room was quickly overshadowed by fear. The nurse handed her a gown and said, "The doctor will be with you shortly."

After her examination Janine met with the doctor in her office. "The news isn't good," the doctor said. "You have a sexually transmitted disease called papillomavirus—HPV for short. It's treatable but not curable." The doctor flipped through her chart. "How old are you?"

"Almost eighteen," said Janine.

The doctor glanced up at her and shook her head. "I have another more serious concern. You have a suspicious-looking growth on your cervix. There are many varieties of STDs, but the one you have is often associated with cervical cancer. I've taken a Pap smear; let's get the results before we go any further."

Janine felt like she was in slow motion as she stood to leave.

"You know," said the doctor, "your personal life is your business, but maybe this is a wake-up call. Maybe it's time to think about the way you're living your life."

Janine said nothing but opened the door and sped down the hall, tears blurring her vision. In the car she released the pent-up sobs. The doctor was right, she did lead a promiscuous life. She supposed she was getting what she deserved.

Janine and her older sister, Diane, were pretty much on their own since their mother and stepfather had moved to a nearby city for new jobs. Diane dealt with her loneliness and fears by attending church; Janine looked for comfort in relationships with boys at school.

She felt dirty, contaminated, and desperately alone. She had no one to talk to—not her mother, her sister, not even a trusted friend.

Less than two weeks later, the doctor called. The Pap was abnormal, indicating severe cell abnormalities. Over the next several weeks and months Janine had a procedure to scrape the lining of the uterus, acid treatments, cryosurgeries to freeze abnormal cells, and periodic biopsies and Paps to monitor the cell growth.

Diane knew something was troubling her younger sister, but she couldn't get her to open up. "Janine, I'm going to church tonight. Why don't you come with me?" Diane asked.

It certainly wasn't the first time her sister had invited her. In fact, it was beginning to get on Janine's nerves. "If I go with you, will you stop bugging me?" she finally said.

The best thing about the church service that night was when her sister introduced her to Tamara. There was something so warm and accepting about her that Janine liked her right away. Apparently the feelings were mutual because a friendship quickly started. Finally, Janine had someone to talk to—someone who could share her heavy load. Yet she still had no interest in returning to church.

At breakfast one morning, Diane said, "There's a play at church tomorrow night. Come with me!" She noticed Janine's brow form a negative furrow. "Tamara will be there!"

The play was called *Heaven's Gates and Hell's Flames*. It was series of short skits about death and the afterlife. Janine was spellbound. In the first one a mother and daughter were driving home from church when they got into a fatal car wreck. But their tragedy on earth ended with joy in heaven as they looked into Jesus' eyes. The next skit portrayed a very different scene. A father and son died in an accident; the son went to heaven and into the arms of his Savior, while the father was confronted with death and eternal separation from his son and from God.

As she watched, Janine realized for the first time in her life that her soul was in jeopardy. She knew it was just a play, but she envied the actors' joy upon seeing the Lord in heaven. She wanted that. She needed that. After the play the audience was invited to come forward and give their lives to Christ and receive him as their Savior. Janine went forward gladly and joyfully.

Immediately, the priorities in her life were rearranged. She understood that now, wherever she went and whatever she did, the Lord was beside her. She couldn't bear the thought of involving him in anything sinful.

Despite this profound change in her life, the effects of her previous behavior clung to her like static. Two weeks later the doctor contacted her again. She wanted to do another cryosurgery. If that was not successful, she would have to do a laser surgery—the last effort before the final option of a hysterectomy.

Janine was stunned at the prospect of a hysterectomy. She had always dreamed of having children. And what man would want a young woman who couldn't give him a family? When she was alone, Janine cried and prayed. She felt that the Lord was comforting her and telling her to endure the treatments, and, eventually, all would bring glory to him.

After the procedure the doctor said, "If the results still aren't good, I'll call you to schedule the laser surgery. If you don't hear from me, all is well."

Janine was at Tamara's house about two months later when she decided to call home and check the messages on her answering machine. Her mouth went dry when she heard the doctor's voice. "Janine, the last Pap still showed a level four cancer. Call immediately and schedule the laser procedure."

Janine was distraught as Tamara drove her home. "I guess I'd hoped that God's grace and mercy would somehow cover the problems that started before I knew him. But he must be telling me that I have to reap what I've sown."

As Janine got out of the car, Tamara said, "Try not to worry. I'll call you tonight."

Janine had just set down her purse and keys when Tamara reappeared at her front door. "I've never done this before," she said, "but I want to lay hands on you and pray."

She took Janine's hand and prayed, "Father, your Word says that when we are in Christ, we are new creations. Please heal Janine's broken spirit and make it new. Amen." She hugged her friend and left.

Although she was touched by Tamara's concern, Janine was a little annoyed by her prayer. Didn't Tamara realize that she needed *physical* healing? She had only prayed for him to heal her broken spirit!

Although the doctor said the procedure was urgent, Janine told Tamara, "I'm not going back to the doctor! I've had enough. I hate going into that horrible place and having her look at me the way she does. I'm not going back!"

But about two months later, Tamara called her and said, "Janine, I think it's time for you to make your doctor appointment."

"No, I told you, I'm not going back."

"I know you don't want to, but I think you need to go anyway, Janine. I really do!"

The following week Janine was reluctantly back on the examining table in the doctor's office.

The doctor looked up. "Have you been to another doctor, Janine?" she asked.

"No," she answered.

"You're telling me," the doctor's voice was unmistakably angry, "that you haven't seen another physician?"

"No, I haven't," said Janine.

"Well, I'm having a hard time believing that! The lump on your cervix isn't there anymore! I'll do another Pap, but I'd like you to tell me the truth! Have you seen another physician?"

Janine was speechless as a deep and certain knowledge gradually seeped into her heart.

"Janine!" the doctor was insistent. "I asked you a question!"

"The only Physician that has touched me other than you is the Great Physician—the Lord!"

From that point forward there has never been evidence of irregular cells or an indication of a sexually transmitted disease in any blood test Janine has had taken.

Years later, she sometimes thinks back to Tamara's prayer. It was certainly led by the Holy Spirit himself, for it says in his Word, "Therefore, if anyone is in Christ, he is a new creation; the old has gone, the new has come!" Only the Lord could make such a claim, and only the Great Physician could heal her—body and soul.

Is This All There Is?

It was the question that was haunting Dean: "Is this all there is to life?"

Not that it hadn't been a good life so far—in fact, it had been very good. He came from a stable, loving family and had gone on to graduate from college with a degree in mechanical engineering. At twenty-five he met Marlene. They fell in love and were married two years later.

The years went by. He had a terrific job that gave them enough income to buy whatever they wanted, his marriage was happy, his four children were thriving, he was in the prime of his life, and his career was soaring.

One day in the coffee room at work, he found himself in a deeply philosophical discussion with a coworker he barely knew.

"So, what do you think, Rick?" asked Dean. "Do you think this is all there is to life?"

Rick laughed. "Wow! Is this a midlife crisis in progress, or what?"

Dean raised his eyebrows. "Could be, but I don't really think so. I've thought about this for a long time. I have everything anyone could possibly want. . . ."

"But?" asked Rick.

"But I'm just not happy."

Dean was suddenly embarrassed. His comment sounded profound and childish at the same time. They were quiet for an awkward moment, and then Dean got up from the table, pushed in his chair, and swung his jacket over his shoulder.

"Well! On that note—I'd better get back to work."

Dean was almost out the door when Rick said in a soft voice, "I know why you're not happy."

He turned back toward Rick. "Pardon me?" Dean said.

"I know why you're not happy."

Dean gave an ironic laugh. "Okay," he playfully glanced at his watch. "I guess I've got another minute—why don't you tell me why I'm not happy."

Rick looked at him levelly. "You don't have a personal relationship with your Creator—with God!"

The smile vanished from Dean's face. He couldn't think of a thing to say. Rick couldn't have said anything that would have confused him more.

Over the next several days Dean thought a great deal about Rick's comments. He knew about God and had gone to church as a child. He remembered hearing sermons about the importance of treating other people well and helping the less fortunate, but he had never heard anyone say anything about having a *relationship* with God. It was a foreign and bewildering concept.

Somehow the busyness of life gradually distracted him from pondering such slippery questions. The years flew by. Suddenly Dean was sixty-two years old and retired. The children were raised and married, and seven grandchildren occasionally repopulated their empty nest with joy. Maybe it was because he had more time to think, but once again came the old, nagging question: "Is this all there is?"

It was Christmastime, and their next-door neighbor stopped by the house and invited them to attend Christmas Eve services with them. It had been years since Dean and Marlene had been to church, but it was Christmas—it sounded like a nice thing to do.

The church was aglow with candlelight and the melodies of familiar carols. To Dean's surprise, instead of a traditional Christmas message, the pastor began talking about having a personal relationship with Jesus Christ. That word again! *Relationship!* The long-ago conversation with his coworker popped up from deep in his memory. He tuned in with interest to the pastor's words.

"Each person is spiritually lost until he admits that he is a sinner and surrenders his life to the Lord," said the pastor

What, Dean wondered, did it mean to "surrender" your life?

He didn't get all his answers that night, but he was definitely curious. He wanted to hear more. So when the New Year rolled around, he and Marlene began attending their neighbor's church on a regular basis. Dean was learning a lot, but he still felt as though he was holding many individual pieces to a puzzle but hadn't yet figured out the big picture.

About three months later the pastor's message seemed to be aimed directly at him: "I know there is someone here today that has been struggling with the idea of completely surrendering his or her life to the Lord. You're on the verge of crossing over the line and giving your all to God, but you haven't yet made your decision."

Dean felt as though a spotlight was on his heart.

The pastor continued. "God wants to have a personal relationship with you! God wants you to cross over the line."

Dean's mind began to race. What would Marlene and the children think? What would their friends think?

"Some of you," the pastor went on, "have felt an emptiness deep inside for many years. You know that the world can't offer anything that will completely fill that emptiness. If you give your life to Christ, your search will be over—your emptiness will finally be filled."

That was it! Dean had found his answer at long last. That day he made the decision to cross the line—to surrender his life to God. He admitted that he was a sinner who had lived his life according to his own wishes. He was ready to get on board with God's plan and purpose—whatever that might be. Although he still didn't know exactly what it meant, he knew he wanted a *relationship* with Jesus Christ.

He began to feel an immediate peace and joy. It was unlike anything he had ever experienced. Not only did his life suddenly have great meaning and purpose; he knew that when his life ended, he would be spending eternity with God!

Marlene was happy for Dean's spiritual change, but she wasn't ready to make the same decision. But just three months later, she found out for herself what it meant to have a personal relationship with Jesus Christ.

One of Dean's greatest joys came when he led each of his four children to the Lord. Even though he had achieved financial and professional success in his lifetime, he knew that this was the work he had been especially called to accomplish!

Despite the necessary losses and health problems that have accompanied growing older, the ten years since Dean and Marlene made their decisions to follow Christ have been the best years of their lives. Looking back, Dean sometimes regrets the years spent without the joy of a relationship with God, but that is outweighed by his thankfulness that the Lord was patient with him.

He wonders if his comfortable and successful-looking life might have been the biggest obstacle to seeing his own need for a Savior. Thank goodness, the Lord continued to pester him with that one, unanswered question: "Is this all there is?"

All those years ago, his coworker, Rick, had the answer when he said, "Until you know your Creator, you'll never be happy."

It took Dean a while to figure that one out. But he knows this is one time when it's truly better late than never!

Looking Back on Lessons Learned

- Man is meant to know his Creator. There's an empty place in our hearts that can only be filled with a relationship with Jesus Christ.
- Having questions about God is okay. However, each person is responsible for seeking out the answers.
- It's tempting to let the mundane demands of the world to distract us from the eternally important issues.
- A house divided against itself cannot stand, and divided beliefs weaken our foundation in life.
- Is this present life all there is to life? Not even close!
- Love is a choice and a decision. Choosing to love God with our whole heart is a decision that affects every aspect of our life: mind, body, and soul.
- The most important choice of life is choosing to follow Jesus Christ. Faith will follow. It is where belief and actions meet.
- The decision to receive Jesus into our lives is a step through a narrow doorway that leads to a wide, deep, and profoundly rewarding life.
- We are either for or against Jesus. There is no middle ground.
- A philosophy, belief system, relaxation method, or religion cannot love us, care for us, lead us, or die for our sins.
- Knowing we are lost without God is the first step to being found.
- As long as we are alive, it's not too late to come to Christ.
- Building a home requires a solid foundation. Building a life that reaches into eternity requires a foundation in Christ.

11

You've Got Your Father's Eyes

Because you are sons, God sent the Spirit
of his Son into our hearts, the Spirit
who calls out, "Abba, Father."
GALATIANS 4:6

Have you ever come before God with a heavy heart? Maybe your problem was so confusing and complex that you sat numbly in God's presence unable to formulate your thoughts or know what you should ask. Perhaps all you could do was read your Bible and quietly weep.

Amazingly, our loving Father has made provision for us during the most trying and baffling of circumstances. At the moment we humbly come to him in prayer, the Holy Spirit begins to mediate for us with "groans that words cannot express" (Rom. 8:26). What a comfort! Like a close friend who listens to your concerns and responds by saying, "I'll pray for you," it feels wonderful to know that someone who understands and cares for you will speak to God on your behalf.

Now, consider that the Holy Spirit, who understands us perfectly because he indwells us, prays for us perfectly in God's will because he is God! This incredible intercessory prayer is just one of the Holy Spirit's functions in the life of a believer.

Even before we receive Christ as our Savior, the Holy Spirit is already at work in our lives, drawing us and making us aware of our need for God. It is not our natural human inclination either to see our own sin or the light of the gospel (see 2 Cor. 4:4). Knowing this, Jesus told his disciples about the coming of the Holy Spirit and how he would make men aware of their sin.

*"When he [the Holy Spirit] comes, he will convict the world of
guilt in regard to sin and righteousness and judgment: in
regard to sin, because men do not believe in me; in regard to
righteousness, because I am going to the Father, where you
can see me no longer; and in regard to judgment, because the
prince of this world now stands condemned." (John 16:8–11)*

As the Holy Spirit works in our lives, our spiritual blinders are
removed, and we are able to see our need for God. Therefore, the Holy
Spirit is deeply involved in our regeneration and renewal when we are born again
(Titus 3:5). After we have taken that all-important step to ask Jesus into our
hearts, the Holy Spirit is there to reassure us that we are, indeed, children of God.

> *If God has
> made your cup
> sweet, drink it with
> grace; if he has
> made it bitter, drink
> it in communion
> with him.*
> —OSWALD CHAMBERS

*The Spirit himself testifies
with our spirit that we are God's
children. (Rom. 8:16)*

This comfort and assurance of our
security and love as a child of God can
be a difficult truth to grasp. But because the Holy Spirit resides in each
believer, he is able to know our deepest, unspoken concerns and graciously answers them. In the following story, the Holy Spirit compassionately replaced doubt with a very personal form of assurance and
security.

Many years ago as a new believer, Kyra struggled with one particular issue of faith. She knew she loved the Lord, but she had trouble
understanding and accepting that he loved her as an individual. She
secretly doubted that Jesus could uniquely and personally love her
when he had so many children and she was so unremarkable.

It was during this period that Kyra had a dream. She dreamed she
was in Jerusalem in the midst of a huge crowd. She gasped when she
heard murmuring that Jesus was coming. She knew that she *had* to see
him. On tiptoe, she looked across the throng to the massive wall that
separated them from the road where the Lord would be passing by.
There was one small doorway leading to the other side, and people
were slowly funneling through.

Shamelessly she pushed, squirmed, and edged through the crowd—at times crawling on her hands and knees through the sea of legs. When she finally scrambled near the door, the voices on the other side swelled in excitement as Jesus came into their view. But with only inches to go, she stumbled and fell, scraping her lip on the rough jamb of the door.

In the frenzy, people pushed her down and stepped on her when she tried to get to her feet. Finally, she huddled against the wall tasting the mixture of tears and blood from her wound. Her heart was sick with disappointment; after being so close, she would miss seeing the Lord.

Immediately, Jesus was at her side. He stooped next to her, and the clamor ceased. At that moment, the world consisted only of his face, which defined compassion and love. With concern in his eyes, he reached out and touched her bleeding lip with his fingertips, healing it instantly.

She was unable to speak but thought to herself, *Why would you even care about something so minor as a cut on my lip?* He smiled and said, "My sweet child—because I love you."

Jesus' touch assured her that the Lord was capable of loving her intimately and individually—as though she were the only person in the world. And he chose the most private place of all to tell her so— in her dream.

This is the work of a loving, approachable, and immensely compassionate God. Unfortunately, many believers are unclear and uncomfortable in their limited understanding of Holy Spirit. Perhaps the third Person of the Trinity seems vague and elusive in part because of his name: Holy *Spirit*, Holy *Ghost*. How do we relate to this Person who is sometimes portrayed as breath, or wind? The other two Persons of the Trinity are somehow easier to know: God the Father is sensed in creation; God the Son in the Person of Jesus Christ; but God the Holy Spirit seems to be outside our familiar realm of understanding. However, in addition to his godly attributes, the Bible reveals him as One who possesses many identifiable traits such as leading (Rom. 8:14), guiding (John 16:13), possessing the ability to be grieved (Eph. 4:30), and comforting (John 15:26).

These traits often come to our attention in subtle and unusual ways. It's ironic that sometimes when we have a special, pressing need for guidance, God can seem far away and even unconcerned. Frequently we pray with expectations that our prayers will be answered in a particular way. At these times, the Holy Spirit may be drawing us into a more mature and trusting union with himself—rather than a relationship that hinges on God doing what we tell him to do.

> The Holy Spirit is the divine substitute on earth today for the bodily presence of the Lord Jesus Christ two thousand years ago.
> —ALAN REDPATH

Laura's mother hadn't felt well for months. The doctors were puzzled when all the initial tests appeared normal, but then a CAT scan revealed the problem: a tumor was growing near her stomach. Naturally, the next question was whether or not the tumor was cancerous. Immediately, the doctor scheduled an exploratory surgery for the following Monday. Laura flew in on Thursday night to be with her mom through the preoperative testing in the days prior to surgery.

The night she arrived, they sat up late praying and reading passages of faith and healing from the Bible. Laura took comfort in those verses from Scripture, but in the midst of such frightening circumstances, she felt painfully ignorant of God's plan for healing. She knew that while some people in the Bible were healed, others lived with the pain and struggle of ongoing illness. Laura wanted to make certain that they were taking all the faithful action that God would have them take.

Her prayer was a simple one, "Father, I pray that Mom doesn't have cancer. Be our Guide and lead us through these difficult times."

The next morning was spent at the hospital with preoperative testing. Afterwards, when they pulled into the driveway, they noticed a piece of paper fluttering near the edge of the lawn. Her mother picked it up and studied it. "Look at this!"

In her hand she held a single page torn from a small New Testament. Immediately, they recognized one of the verses they had read the night before: James 5:14 which says, "Is any one of you sick?

He should call the elders of the church to pray over him and anoint him with oil in the name of the Lord."

They placed the page on the kitchen table and talked about it. Neither of them had a Bible that size. Could this unusual incident be God's leading? Maybe because they were accustomed to dealing with their problems privately, it took courage for them to place that call to the elders. But they did. They felt immediate comfort and encouragement to know that others were praying on their behalf as Laura's mom faced her surgery. And afterwards, when they learned that the tumor was indeed cancer, prayers from other people were especially needed and appreciated.

It wouldn't be truthful to say that Laura wasn't disappointed and confused with the diagnosis. She had pictured a miraculous deliverance *from* this dreaded disease. Now, thirteen years later, having exceeded the most optimistic prognosis, it's clear that God chose instead to deliver her mom *through* it.

Sometimes Laura thinks about that odd and thrilling moment of finding that single, significant page from a little Bible—it was a marker of light left for them on a dark and twisting path by an ever-faithful Guide.

We struggle with the dilemma of *how* to lead the Christian life when we are constantly bombarded by the cares and pressures of the world. We know we can't do it on our own strength. Jesus said, "And I will ask the Father, and he will give you another Counselor to be with you forever" (John 14:16). The Holy Spirit is the answer.

> *Whether we preach, pray, write, do business, travel, take care of children or administer the government— whatever we do—our whole life and influence should be filled with the power of the Holy Spirit.*
> —CHARLES G. FINNEY

The analogy has been aptly made that a home may be wired with electricity, but it is useless until we plug into its power and put it to use. Similarly, learning behaviors and skills for making good decisions and living a full life must include plugging into the Holy Spirit's role in our lives through prayer, submission, and guidance. Because the Holy Spirit lives in every believer and promises to guide us into all truth (John 16:13), we have great power and guidance at our fingertips.

CALL UPON HIM

It was New Year's Eve of 1942. Ray was a twenty-two-year-old petty officer first class stationed in Perth, Australia, at the seaport of Free Mantle. World War II was raging, and Ray was smack in the middle of it. He was in charge of the engine room that ran the 305-foot submarine, the USS *Tambor*.

Their mission was to locate and intercept Japanese merchant ships that were en route to the Philippines and other Japanese islands. Although the mission was routine, he had learned early on that there was no such thing as a routine war patrol.

The sub moved silently through the Lombok Straits near Bali. The captain had decided on this route through the short and shallow passages as a means of saving time and hopefully intercepting the Japanese convoy expected in that area.

"'Battle Stations Torpedo!' The captain's order quickened Ray's pulse and sent all fourteen men in the engine room into a flurry of activity. A convoy had been spotted consisting of three Japanese merchant ships and their escort. Under the cover of night, the sub made a surface approach.

One at a time all six torpedoes were fired from the bow tubes. The sub was then turned 180 degrees to fire the four torpedoes from the stern tubes. Two torpedoes were fired, sinking the third merchant ship.

Success, however, was short-lived. The escort, a Japanese destroyer loaded with antisub warfare, had been out of range of their torpedoes. And now it began a deadly approach on them.

The klaxon horn sounded three piercing blows instructing the men to diving stations. Ray gave the order to secure the engines for dive. Working furiously, they shut down the engines and closed the valves. Because the sub was still in the shallow area outside the straits, they were able to descend only seventy-eight feet.

The escort crossed above, echo ranging them with pings from its sonar in an effort to pinpoint the sub's position. The grim reality of the situation was becoming clear to Ray. Retaliation would be suicide in view of the escort's weapons. They couldn't run; the resulting wake would only identify their location, and in these shallow waters they couldn't submerge deep enough to hide. They were trapped!

The men could hear the approach of the escort's engines and the click of a depth charge as it armed prior to exploding on impact with the ship. A depth charge was the most destructive when it fell beneath a sub. It would explode sideways first and then up, shattering the hull and quickly sinking the ship. But because the sub was sitting directly on the ocean floor, the depth charges were landing on top of the sub and pounding it onto the ground.

For hours the assault continued. Radio contact was lost, and the ship rocked wildly. Ray wondered how many hits the sub could withstand before it cracked open and sent all eighty-five men to their watery grave. Water leaked in. The crew tightened valves and fittings, doing their best to make repairs between hits from the destroyer.

Hours drug into days. It had been two and one half days since the attack began. It seemed impossible that the sub hadn't broken apart. The relentless pounding was torture. The men worked and waited silently. Sound carries through water, so unnecessary talking could give away their position.

Ray sat down on the deck plate with his head resting in his hands and prayed. Like all fighting men, Ray lived with his own private fears. But unlike many of his shipmates, Ray had a relationship with Jesus Christ. Prayer had taken on new meaning since he'd been in the war; it was a vital link to God and his hope of survival. If he died, he was ready to meet his Maker, but he had a deep faith that God would see him through the worst.

"Lord," he prayed, "I know you're here. Otherwise we'd already be dead. The Bible says to call upon you in days of trouble and you will deliver me. I'm doing that—I'm calling upon you. Save us, Father."

One of his shipmates sat down beside him. His face dripped with sweat from the 100-plus degree temperature in the compartment. "What are you doing, Ray?" he whispered.

Ordinarily, he might not have told him the truth. "I'm praying, Jimmy."

"Do you think it will do any good? It pretty much looks like we've had it."

"Yeah, but nothing is impossible with God." Ray looked at him. "Why don't you pray?"

Jimmy studied his hands, "Heck, I've never been much for prayin' . . . ."

Ray smiled at him. "Well, seems like a pretty good time to start."

The hours wore on and the attack continued: sixty hours, seventy, seventy-two. Ray could hear the hum of the Japanese warship's motor. It was a pattern that was becoming all too familiar. The sound was intense as it crossed directly overhead, then it gradually faded until the ship turned and approached them again to deliver another blow.

Was he imagining it, or did the motor's hum sound farther away this time? He strained to hear. Silence. The men looked into each other's eyes, but no one dared speak. The attack had ended—but why?

The crew turned their efforts toward getting the battered sub operational. It was then that they discovered what had kept the sub from being shattered. The depth charges had pounded them into the soft ocean floor, burrowing the sub into a muddy nest that protected them from the force of the blows. Eventually, the depth charges had ruptured a fuel tank that sent up an oil slick. At that point, the Japanese escort must have taken it as evidence that they had sunk the sub.

The attack on the USS *Tambor* was over, but their problems weren't. The same mud that had protected them now held them in a fierce suction. For four hours, under the sharp command of the captain, they rocked the sub back and forth by pumping water from the bow tanks back into the stern. When the sub tilted, the captain would start the propellers. Little by little, they inched upward until the sub finally broke free of the suction.

The attack had taken an incredible toll on the ship. The huge conning tower had been knocked six inches off center, and only one engine out of four was operational. Every glass, lightbulb, porcelain fixture, and mirror had been broken, rendering them "blind"—unable to use the periscopes. Amazingly, despite the loss of fuel, an adequate supply remained, and they limped home.

Back at their seaport, word of their ordeal and miraculous survival spread like wildfire. They had been presumed lost.

In the years to come, the memory of that incident would sustain Ray through many of life's problems and challenges. There would be other times of trouble when the odds were stacked against him, but he had learned one lesson very well: When you call upon God, odds don't mean a thing.

BREATHING LESSONS

Life on the farm suited Jan and her husband, Fred. It was not a leisurely existence, but she had been raised on the principles of diligence, self-reliance, and hard work. She was comfortable when they were required of her. As a child, her father would settle for nothing less than the best from her, and she learned early on that to avoid conflict with him, she had to work things out on her own.

She took a similar approach in dealing with God. "God helps those who help themselves" was the single motto that influenced her as a child and defined her as an adult. She figured that God was probably a lot like her father. If she did her best to stay on the straight and narrow, God wouldn't have any reason to get involved or punish her for doing something wrong.

When Fred and Jan's daughter, Sara, was born, Jan's love for her baby was so fierce that it almost frightened her. She was determined to raise her child well and protect her from the dangers of life. If something tough got in Jan's way or threatened her child, she would be tougher—she would be stronger—and meaner if necessary. One way or another she would prevail.

Jan was cooking supper one evening as two-year-old Sara played on the floor in the kitchen. Sara came up beside Jan and tugged on her skirt.

"Are you hungry, sweetie?" asked Jan.

Sara nodded her head and laughed. "Cheese!"

Jan cut off a chunk from the block of cheese and handed it to Sara for her to nibble on. She turned back to chopping vegetables, but in a moment, she heard Sara making an odd gasping sound. Her little girl had not nibbled on the cheese as Jan had expected; instead, she had put the whole thing in her mouth! Now she was choking and turning blue.

Jan dropped to her knees and stuck her index finger down Sara's throat groping for the cheese. She couldn't even touch it. Over and over she tried until her knuckle bled from scraping against Sara's teeth. She grabbed her baby and turned her upside down, thumping her repeatedly on the back, but it wouldn't dislodge.

"Fred! Fred!" she called. She knew he was home, but she had no idea where he was. He could be anywhere on the farm.

She ran toward the phone. *911—I'll call 911!*

But then she remembered last spring when a horse had thrown her; it took the ambulance over an hour to find their farm. She didn't have an hour! She grabbed her keys. She would drive Sara to the hospital herself. Normally it was about a twenty-minute drive—maybe she could get there in ten.

Sara was still clutching at her throat and gagging as Jan ran in the garage with her in her arms. Thankfully, Fred was there sharpening tools.

"Get in the truck!" yelled Jan. "We have to take Sara to the hospital; she's choking to death! Hurry!"

Fred jumped in the driver's side and they sped down the road.

Jan looked down at Sara. She was no longer gagging and fighting. She had gone limp in her arms.

"Oh, my God! O, my God!" cried Jan. "Fred—faster! Drive faster! Hurry! She's dying!"

Suddenly, Jan knew with crushing certainty that there was nothing she could do to save her daughter.

"Oh, God, please help us! Save our baby!" Her cry for help came from the untouched depths of her soul.

Sobbing, she cradled and rocked Sara on her lap. Her daughter's limp body suddenly convulsed. The toddler gagged and coughed. At last she dragged in a ragged breath that erupted in a beautiful life-affirming wail!

Fred pulled the car to the side of the road, and they frantically inspected their daughter. They could only guess that the jerking of the convulsion dislodged the cheese from her throat. She was still crying, and she looked all right, but they decided to go on to the hospital and have her checked.

At the hospital she was examined carefully, but the doctor assured them that their daughter was fine. Several hours after the ordeal began, they returned home. Sara had fallen asleep in the car, and Jan carried her into her room and placed her in the crib. For a long time she and Fred watched her as she slept. They were speechless with emotion and gratitude.

Fred fell into an exhausted sleep, but as tired as she was, Jan could not wind down. Her thoughts and feelings tumbled over each other in confusion. Finally, she put on her robe and slippers and walked outside under the night sky. Jan paced up and down their country road looking at the stars, trying to ponder the God who had placed them in the heavens.

Like those far-off stars, she realized that all her life she had tried to keep God at a safe distance. She wouldn't bother him if he didn't bother her. But today he had brought her to the point where she had reached the end of herself. Her long-held philosophy that God helps those that help themselves crumbled before her eyes. At a time when she could do nothing to help her dying child, God had brought her a merciful miracle.

On that starlit, country road, Jan looked up to the heavens and wept.

"I'm so sorry, Lord! All my life, I've thought you were just waiting to zap me if I messed up. I thought you were my worst enemy, and now I see that you're my best Friend. I've ignored you all my life, but when I called on you, you still loved me and answered my desperate prayer! I don't want to be on my own anymore. I want to know you— I want to love you!"

The change in Jan was gradual but absolute. The dusty Bible came off the shelf. She read it hungrily, breathing in the words of her Savior and letting them bring life to the empty places in her heart.

Jan is still a realist; she knows that in this life bad things sometimes happen. But now she knows she doesn't have to be tough and rely only on herself. On her own her daughter would have died. But God was there. He breathed life back into the lifeless body of her child, and at the same time, he breathed his strong and patient love into her life.

Carol flinched at the sound of the ringing phone. Lately the telephone had become a resident enemy—a means for Larry to harass her and tell her how good his life was now that they were no longer married.

"Carol, how are you?"

She was flooded with relief. "Patti! I'm so glad it's you. I miss you so much!"

"You've been on my mind, Carol. Are you all right? I've been worried about you."

There was nothing quite so comforting as the sound of her best friend's voice. They had met in their church youth group when they were in junior high school, and a bond quickly developed. They called themselves "eternal friends" and vowed to always try to live near each other. Through the years the strong friendship had endured, but Patti's marriage to a man in the Air Force uprooted her and took her all over the country and thousands of miles away. In spite of the distance, Patti could always sense when Carol was depressed.

Carol knew there was no point in trying to sound upbeat. "It's hard, Patti. Larry calls constantly and never misses a chance to put me down. Sometimes he's drunk, and it's as though he's just trying to make things difficult for the kids and me. He hasn't sent any money in weeks. I'm worried we might lose the house."

"Oh, Carol, I'm so sorry."

Carol went on, "You know how long it's been since I've worked, but now I've got to find a job. I worry about leaving the kids; they need me so much right now, but I don't have a choice." She couldn't hold back the tears. "I try to pray, but it's hard for me to remember that God cares—I feel so lonely, and he seems so far away. How I wish you lived nearby! Pray for me, Patti."

"I will—you know I will. I'll get my prayer group to pray for you."

Weeks passed. Carol was relieved to find a job, but little else had changed. The weekdays were a blur of rushing and responsibilities. Saturdays and Sundays were a brief respite before it started all over again.

One Saturday the kids were at a friend's, and Carol found herself alone. The house was unusually quiet as she went about the business of doing laundry and tending to chores that had been neglected through the week. As she walked down the hallway toward the kitchen, a profoundly peaceful feeling enveloped her. It so overwhelmed her that she stopped and leaned against the wall. In the utter stillness, she heard voices—murmuring voices. Although she couldn't make out any words, there was a gentle tone to the sounds that made the odd experience comforting rather than alarming. She stood still and let the voices wash over her. After a while the sound faded but the unusual feeling of peace remained for days to come.

Patti called about a week later. After they had caught up on news, Patti said, "I've been praying for you," she said. "Last Saturday our prayer group got together especially to pray for you."

With a little gasp Carol asked, "What time was that?"

Taking into account the time difference, it turned out that Patti's prayer group was praying at the exact time Carol heard the soft voices and experienced the delightful peace.

They quietly pondered this. Finally Patti said, "You know, I think God wanted you to know that even when it doesn't feel like it, he's always near."

"Yes," said Carol, and then she added, "and maybe he also wanted to remind me that it takes more than a few time zones to separate eternal friends."

Surrendering All

It began as a mother's uneasy feeling.

Debbie studied her eight-year-old son and then asked her mom, "Do you think Stephen's stomach looks distended—you know—unusually large?"

His grandmother looked at her grandson. "I think he looks just fine."

Debbie tried to feel reassured, but she didn't.

The next day, in the car on the way home from church, Debbie turned around and looked at Stephen. His breathing seemed labored, and she asked him if he was feeling all right.

"I'm just a little tired," he said.

The concern continued, so on Monday Debbie called the doctor and made an appointment. The doctor examined Stephen and thought that his liver might be enlarged. "Whatever it is," he said, "we need to find out. Let's run some tests."

The next day the family was having pizza at a restaurant when Debbie got a call from the doctor on their cell phone. "Can you and your husband come in this afternoon? We need to discuss the test results," he said.

They dropped Stephen at his grandmother's and hurried to the office. The doctor was somber. "It's serious," he said. "I think he may have a tumor the size of a grapefruit near his bladder." He had already contacted a pediatric oncologist and arranged for a room for them at the Ronald McDonald House in Portland, Oregon.

It wasn't until they arrived that the full reality of the situation began to sink in. At the admissions desk, Debbie made the comment that they were fortunate that a room was available on such short notice. The woman smiled and said, "Well, cancer patients have top priority."

Cancer! It was the first time the word had been spoken. Debbie and Terry were numb with worry. That night Debbie felt as though her world was crashing in on her. How could their child have cancer? She had always prided herself on being a good mother. How could a good mother not have a healthy child?

On Monday, surrounded by family and friends, Stephen was wheeled into an operating room for an exploratory surgery. Debbie and Terry prayed and asked that God's will would be done in their son's life. In spite of the frightening circumstances, they felt a sense of peace.

Following the surgery, their faith was severely tested. The surgeon told them that Stephen had multiple tumors from his diaphragm down.

"Were you able to remove them?" Terry asked.

The doctor shook his head. "Because the tumors are on or near vital organs, we weren't able to remove them without risking further harm. However, we removed five inches of his intestines that were blocked with tumors."

Debbie wiped her eyes. "What is it—what does he have?"

"It will take a couple of days to get an exact diagnosis," the doctor said, "but there's no way around it—it looks very serious."

A few days later they learned that Stephen had a rare cancer called Burkitt's lymphoma. If he began chemotherapy immediately, the doctors felt he would have a 40 to 60 percent chance of survival.

The first chemotherapy treatment was hard on Stephen. "Mommy, my tummy hurts," he said, over and over. He was given morphine, but it didn't seem to help very much. When his parents prayed over him, however, there was an obvious lessening of the pain. Even the nurses noticed that the prayers seemed to have the greater effect on him.

Two weeks after the initial surgery, however, his pain was growing increasingly severe. At first the doctors were baffled, but they began to suspect that he had a hole somewhere in his digestive track. Stephen was scheduled for an emergency surgery. The doctors didn't attempt to minimize the seriousness of the situation. They told Debbie and Terry that it was possible that Stephen would die during this long and complex surgery.

Immediately, they got on the phone to family and friends and asked them to call others to begin praying in earnest for Stephen.

As Stephen was being taken in to surgery, Debbie and Terry noticed a young, well-dressed man standing nearby. By now they had been around the hospital long enough that they recognized most of the friends and family members that regularly came and went. But they had never before seen this exceptionally kind-looking young man.

For a long moment the young man thoughtfully and compassionately looked at Stephen. In a sweet, confident voice he turned to Debbie and Terry and said, "I had cancer when I was a child, and now I'm totally cured." He then stepped on the elevator and left. They never saw him again, but his simple message planted a much-needed seed of hope in their hearts.

At 10:00 P.M., Debbie and Terry watched their little boy being taken into surgery, knowing they might never again see him alive. As they began the dreadful task of waiting, Debbie silently prayed, "I surrender my son to you, Lord. I trust you, and I know you understand what I'm feeling, because you surrendered your Son, too."

At a time when it would have been natural to feel utter despair, Debbie felt the overwhelming peace of knowing God himself was in control of the situation. Deep in her spirit she sensed God telling her that Stephen would be all right.

Only two hours later they noticed a patient being wheeled out of the operating room. It couldn't be Stephen; they were anticipating at least five hours of surgery. But to their surprise, Stephen's surgeon approached them, still untying his surgical mask. He sat down beside them and rested his elbows on his knees.

"I can't believe this is the same child I operated on two weeks ago," he said shaking his head. "There are absolutely no visible signs of cancer anywhere!"

Debbie and Terry clutched each other and wept.

When Terry could speak, he asked, "Could it have been the one treatment of chemo?"

The doctor shook his head, "No. It couldn't work that fast."

"What was causing his terrible pain, then?" Debbie asked.

"He had a perforated ulcer—very painful, but very treatable. Fortunately, it's in a location that should not present a risk of infection."

Terry was still trying to process the information. "So, are you saying that Stephen's cancer is in remission?" "No, I'm saying that his cancer is cured! It will likely never come back!"

Debbie and Terry decided to continue the scheduled chemotherapy treatments, not because they didn't believe Stephen was healed, but as an act of obedience.

Stephen is sixteen now and a strong Christian. Every year he goes for checkups, and every year he has received a clean bill of health. Although his memories of that time are sketchy, he knows that God healed him, and he's excited to see what God has in store for the rest of his life.

As Debbie and Terry thought back over the events, they realized that the emergency surgery to repair the perforated ulcer was the only way they could have known what a profound miracle God had performed in their son.

In the face of such extreme circumstances, their faith was tested and stretched in ways they never could have imagined. They discovered that no matter how big or impossible the problem may appear, the God they love and serve can handle it. He is a very big God indeed.

— ▪ —

LOOKING BACK ON LESSONS LEARNED

- Even before we are believers, we are drawn to God through the Holy Spirit. He makes us aware of our need for a Savior, and, after we have received Christ, he reassures us that we are indeed God's children.
- The Holy Spirit listens to our hearts. He understands us perfectly because he indwells us and prays in the perfect will of God because he is God.
- An old saying declares that "God helps those who help themselves." God, however, said nothing of the sort. In fact, he knew our needs so well, he called the Holy Spirit our "Helper."
- In a world beset by lies and deceptions, the Holy Spirit promises to guide us into all truth.
- Believers struggle with how to live the Christian life. The ever-present Holy Spirit is the answer as he counsels us in the way we should go.
- When God doesn't answer our prayers in the way we would like, he is drawing us into a more mature and trusting relationship.
- When we are trying to sort through difficult or confusing decisions, praying for God's will for our lives brings peace out of chaos.
- In times of doubt and hardship, recalling God's past blessings strengthens our faith.
- Regardless of the size of the challenge we may be facing, when we call upon God, the odds don't mean a thing. No matter how big the problem, God is bigger.
- One of our fundamental fears is of being alone. As believers we have God's certain promise that he will never leave us or forsake us.

Underneath It All:
Some Concluding Thoughts

For no one can lay any foundation
other than the one already laid,
which is Jesus Christ.
1 CORINTHIANS 3:11

*I*n the early morning hours of August 24, 1992, Hurricane Andrew traversed southern Florida in a three-hour rampage of destruction. Across the nation television broadcast images of trees being ripped from the ground and homes collapsing in torrents of rain and wind. In spite of the ongoing news coverage, the aftermath of the storm brought the shocking revelation that 180,000 people had been left homeless.

Before Andrew, South Florida hadn't had a significant hurricane in twenty years. Lulled by the years of calm weather, countless new homes had been built in volatile coastal areas, disregarding proper foundation and high-wind construction methods.

Of course, the storm eventually came, and those poorly constructed homes suffered extensive damage or were demolished. Hurricane Andrew has the distinction of being one of the most costly storms in history.

VICARIOUS LESSONS

Witnessing the wrath of a hurricane will motivate most people to try and learn its lessons from a safe distance. Similarly, the wise take advantage of opportunities to learn about life's challenges from others who have already been there. The stories in the preceding chapters have provided such an opportunity. Through them, we've explored topics such as success, life goals, marriage, parenting, friendship, money, regrets, and the search to find the true meaning of life. We have shared experiences that have revealed either a firm foundation in life or one that was based on shallow or faulty beliefs.

People are naturally curious about other people. But more than mere curiosity unites the stories presented between the covers of this book. In these diverse situations and circumstances, one common factor underlies them all—the need for a life built on the foundation of a personal relationship with Jesus Christ.

"Therefore everyone who hears these words of mine and
puts them into practice is like a wise man who built his
house on the rock. The rain came down, the streams rose,
and the winds blew and beat against that house; yet it did not fall,
because it had its foundation on the rock." (Matt. 7:24–25)

ARE WE SEEKING AND LISTENING TO WISE COUNSEL?

Since Hurricane Andrew, Florida and other hurricane-prone areas have taken heed and tried to benefit from the lessons left in the rubble of the storm. Many regions have responded by adopting stricter building codes and renewing their commitment to enforce them. There has also been a reevaluation of low-cost flood insurance, which may encourage people to rebuild their homes and businesses in hazardous locations. Perhaps of greatest value is the emphasis on the wise measures homeowners can take to prepare themselves and their homes for future storms.

The pursuit of wisdom is in itself an act of wisdom. God rewarded Solomon for his request to discern what is right. In our time, many people worship knowledge but regard wisdom as a relative commodity based on individual perceptions of right and wrong. However, there has never been a better time to seek true wisdom and wise counsel. Whether seeking alone or with the help of godly men and women, we must always make sure that the counsel we receive is consistent with the Word of God. Regardless of what we are facing in life, the Bible is an unfailing and unerring source of guidance.

ARE WE PRACTICING OUR BELIEFS?

Intellectual knowledge must be translated into action and behavior before it has any real value in our lives. For instance, someone living in a coastal area may genuinely believe that their home should be retrofitted with extra structural safety measures such as a larger concrete slab, reinforced doors, strong windows, and sturdy shingles on the roof. But if no steps are taken to implement these elements into their home, that knowledge and belief are of no value. They would face the next storm with a head full of knowledge while their house blows away!

> *"But everyone who hears these words of mine and does not*
> *put them into practice is like a foolish man who built his*
> *house on sand. The rain came down, the streams rose, and*
> *the winds blew and beat against that house, and it fell*
> *with a great crash." (Matt. 7:26–27)*

The person who hears the Word of God but fails to obey has not only robbed himself of the abundant life God has planned for him, but exposes himself to many of life's problems. The Bible tells us that a foolish person knows the right thing to do but doesn't do it. Therefore, we should ask ourselves if we are faithfully constructing our daily life in a way that is consistent with God's principles and commands. Obedient action is the very heart of faith.

IS OUR FOUNDATION BUILT ON THE ROCK?

Imagine a lovely home situated on exquisite beachfront property with a breathtaking view of the ocean. For years the family living there felt secure, and passersby admired the home. But the storm came, and the winds lifted it off the sand and shattered it into a thousand pieces. Although once a lovely home, it lacked the most vital structural element: a deep, solid foundation.

A home can be replaced, but our lives are irreplaceable. Now is the time to make sure we are prepared for the inevitable choices and challenges. Jesus himself warned us of the difficult nature of our life on earth so we would be aware that no one is exempt from the storms of life.

> *"I have told you these things, so that in me you may have peace.*
> *In this world you will have trouble." (John 16:33)*

Although the threat of trouble is always sobering, believers can face it knowing our peace is firmly rooted in his divine presence, plan, and power. Standing firm with him, we can have confidence that the winds of adversity will not overtake us. Jesus went on to give us an incredible reassurance:

"But take heart! I have overcome the world." (John 16:33)

Being prepared for life doesn't mean we must be able to overcome the world by our own might; we need only place our faith in the One who has. This is the glorious lesson that surpasses all others.